# a genocide foretold

## ALSO BY CHRIS HEDGES

*Our Class: Trauma and Transformation in an American Prison*

*America: The Farewell Tour*

*Unspeakable* (with David Talbot)

*Wages of Rebellion: The Moral Imperative of Revolt*

*War Is a Force That Gives Us Meaning*

*Days of Destruction, Days of Revolt* (with Joe Sacco)

*The World As It Is: Dispatches on the Myth of Human Progress*

*Death of the Liberal Class*

*Empire of Illusion: The End of Literacy and the Triumph of Spectacle*

*When Atheism Becomes Religion: America's New Fundamentalists*

*Collateral Damage: America's War Against Iraqi Civilians*
(with Laila Al-Arian)

*American Fascists: The Christian Right and the War on America*

*Losing Moses on the Freeway: The 10 Commandments in America*

*What Every Person Should Know About War*

*The Greatest Evil Is War*

# a genocide foretold

reporting on survival and
resistance in occupied palestine

# CHRIS HEDGES

SEVEN STORIES PRESS
NEW YORK ✷ OAKLAND ✷ LONDON

Seven Stories Press
140 Watts Street
New York, NY 10013
www.sevenstories.com

Library of Congress Cataloging-in-Publication Data

Names: Hedges, Chris, author.
Title: A genocide foretold : reporting on survival and resistance in
    occupied Palestine / Chris Hedges.
Description: New York : Seven Stories Press, 2025. | Includes
    bibliographical references.
Identifiers: LCCN 2024050555 | ISBN 9781644214855 (trade paperback) | ISBN
    9781644214862 (ebook)
Subjects: LCSH: Palestinian Arabs--Gaza Strip. | Palestinian Arabs--West
    Bank. | Gaza Strip--History--Bombardment, 2023- | Gaza
    Strip--History--21st century. | West Bank--History--21st century.
Classification: LCC DS110.G3 H44 2025 | DDC 956.94/3055--dc23/eng/20241214
LC record available at https://lccn.loc.gov/2024050555

College professors and high school and middle school teachers may order free examination copies of Seven Stories Press titles. Visit https://www.sevenstories.com/pg/resources-academics or email academic@sevenstories.com.

Printed in the USA.

9 8 7 6 5 4 3 2 1

# CONTENTS

*All I possess in the presence of death*
*Is pride and fury.*[1]

—MAHMOUD DARWISH

# THE OLD EVIL

*Ramallah*
*West Bank, Occupied Palestine*

It comes back in a rush, the stench of raw sewage, the groan of the diesel, sloth-like Israeli armored personnel carriers, the vans filled with broods of children driven by chalky-faced colonists, certainly not from here, probably from Brooklyn or somewhere in Russia, or maybe Britain. Little has changed. The checkpoints, with their blue and white Israeli flags, dot the roads and intersections. The red-tiled roofs of the colonist settlements—illegal under international law—dominate hillsides above Palestinian villages and towns. They have grown in number and expanded in size. But they remain protected by blast barriers, concertina wire, and watchtowers surrounded by the obscenity of lawns and gardens. In this arid landscape, the colonists have access to bountiful sources of water that the Palestinians are denied.[2]

The winding twenty-six-foot high concrete wall that runs the 440-mile length of occupied Palestine, with its graffiti calling for liberation, murals with the Al-Aqsa Mosque, faces of martyrs, and the grinning and bearded mug of Yasser Arafat—whose concessions to Israel in the Oslo Accords made him, in the words of Edward Said, "the Pétain of the Palestinians"—gives the West Bank the feel of an open-air prison.[3] The wall lacerates the landscape. It twists and turns like some huge, fossilized antediluvian snake, severing Palestinians from their families, slicing Palestinian villages in half, cutting communities off from their orchards, olive trees, and fields, dipping and rising out of wadis, trapping Palestinians in the Jewish state's updated version of a Bantustan.

It has been over two decades since I reported from the West Bank. Time collapses. The smells, sensations, emotions, and images, the lilting cadence of Arabic, and the miasma of sudden and violent death that lurks in the air evoke the old evil. It is as if I never left.

I am in a battered black Mercedes driven by a friend in his thirties whom I will not name to protect him. He worked in construction in Israel but lost his job—like nearly all Palestinians employed in Israel—on October 7, 2023. He has four children. He is struggling. His savings have dwindled. It is getting hard to buy food and pay for electricity, water, and petrol. He feels under siege. He *is* under siege. He has little use for the quisling Palestinian Authority. He dislikes Hamas. He has Jewish friends. He speaks Hebrew. The siege is grinding him—and everyone around him—down.

"A few more months like this and we're finished," he says puffing nervously on a cigarette. "People are desperate. More and more are going hungry."

Israel has suspended financial transfers to the Palestinian Authority, which nominally governs the West Bank in collaboration with Israel. It has revoked 148,000 work permits for those who had jobs in Israel. The gross domestic product (GDP) of the West Bank has contracted by 22.7 percent, nearly 30 percent of businesses have closed, and 292,000 jobs have been lost. "Over 692 Palestinians—10 times the previous 14 years' annual average of 69 fatalities—have been killed and more than 5,000 have been injured. Of the 169 Palestinian children who have been killed, nearly 80 percent were shot in the head or the torso," the U.N. reported in October 2024.[4]

We are driving the winding road that hugs the barren sand and scrub hillsides snaking up from Jericho, rising from the salt-rich Dead Sea—the lowest spot on Earth—to Ramallah. I will meet my friend, the novelist Atef Abu Saif, who was in Gaza on October 7 with his fifteen-year-old son, Yasser. They were visiting family when Israel began its scorched-earth campaign. He spent eighty-five days enduring and writing daily about the nightmare of the genocide. His collection of haunting diary entries were published in his book *Don't Look Left*. He escaped the carnage through the border with Egypt at Rafah, traveled to Jordan, and returned home to Ramallah. But the scars of the genocide remain. Yasser rarely leaves his room. He does not engage with his friends. Fear, trauma, and hatred are the primary commodities imparted by the colonizers to the colonized.

"I still live in Gaza," Atef tells me later. "I am not out." Yasser still hears bombing. He still sees corpses. He does not eat meat. Red meat reminds him of the flesh he picked up when he joined the rescue parties during the massacre in Jabaliya, and the flesh of his cousins. "I sleep on a mattress on the floor as I did in Gaza when we lived in a tent. I lie awake. I think of those we left behind waiting for sudden death."

Writing and photographing in wartime are acts of resistance, acts of faith. They affirm the belief that one day—a day the writers, journalists, and photographers may never see—the words and images will evoke empathy, understanding, outrage, and provide wisdom. They chronicle not only the facts, although facts are important, but the texture, sacredness, and grief of lives and communities lost. They tell the world what war is like, how those caught in its maw of death endure, how there are those who sacrifice for others and those who do not, what fear and hunger are like, what death is like. They transmit the cries of children, the wails of grief of mothers, the daily struggle in the face of savage industrial violence, the triumph of humanity over filth, sickness, humiliation, and fear. This is why writers, photographers, and journalists are targeted by aggressors in war—including the Israelis—for obliteration. They stand as witnesses to an evil the aggressors want buried and forgotten. They expose the lies. They condemn, even from the grave, their killers. Israel has killed over two dozen Palestinian poets and writers, along with at least 128 journalists and media workers in Gaza between October 7, 2023 and October 2024.[5]

I experienced futility and outrage when I covered war. I wondered if I had done enough or if it was even worth the risk. But you go on because to do nothing is to be complicit. You report because you care. You make it hard for the killers to deny their crimes.

Atef is no stranger to the violence of the Israeli occupiers. He was two months old during the 1973 war and writes, "I've been living through wars ever since. Just as life is a pause between two deaths, Palestine, as a place and as an idea, is a timeout in the middle of many wars."

During Operation Cast Lead, Israel's 2008–2009 assault on Gaza, Atef sheltered in the corridor of his Gaza family home for twenty-two nights with his wife, Hanna, and two children while Israel bombed and shelled. His book, *The Drone Eats with Me: Diaries from a City Under Fire*, is an account of Operation Protective Edge, the 2014 Israeli assault on Gaza that killed 1,462 Palestinian civilians, including 551 children.

"Memories of war can be strangely positive, because to have them at all means you must have survived," he notes sardonically.

He again did what writers do, including the professor and poet Refaat Alareer, who was killed, along with Refaat's brother, one of his brother's sons, his sister, three of her children and a neighbor, in an airstrike on his sister's apartment building in Gaza on December 7, 2023. The Euro-Mediterranean Human Rights Monitor said that Alareer was deliberately targeted, "surgically bombed out of the entire building."[6] His killing came after weeks of "death threats that Refaat received online and by phone from Israeli accounts." He had moved to his sister's apartment because of the threats. Four months later, Refaat's daughter, Shaima, her husband, and their newborn baby were killed after three Israeli airstrikes struck the home they were sheltering in.

Refaat, whose doctorate was on the metaphysical poet John Donne, wrote a poem called "If I Must Die," which became his last will and testament. He wrote the poem in 2011 and reposted it in November 2023, a month before he was killed. It has been translated into seventy-one languages:

> *If I must die,*
>
> *you must live*
>
> *to tell my story*
>
> *to sell my things*
>
> *to buy a piece of cloth*
>
> *and some strings,*
>
> *(make it white with a long tail)*
>
> *so that a child, somewhere in Gaza*
>
> *while looking heaven in the eye*
>
> *awaiting his dad who left in a blaze—*
>
> *and bid no one farewell*
>
> *not even to his flesh*
>
> *not even to himself—*

*sees the kite, my kite you made, flying up above*

*and thinks for a moment an angel is there*

*bringing back love*

*If I must die*

*let it bring hope*

*let it be a tale*[7]

Atef, once again finding himself living amid the explosions and carnage from Israeli shells and bombs, doggedly published his observations and reflections. His accounts were often difficult to transmit because of Israel's blackout of internet and phone service.

On the first day of the Israeli bombardment, a friend, the young poet and musician Omar Abu Shawish, is killed.

Atef wonders about the Israeli soldiers watching him and his family with "their infrared lenses and satellite photography." Can "they count the loafs of bread in my basket, or the number of falafel balls on my plate?" he asks. He watches the crowds of dazed and confused families, their homes in rubble, carrying "mattresses, bags of clothes, food, and drink." He stands mutely before "the supermarket, the bureau de change, the falafel shop, the fruit stalls, the perfume parlor, the sweets shop, the toy shop—all burned."[8]

"Blood was everywhere, along with bits of kids' toys, cans from the supermarket, smashed fruit, broken bicycles, and shattered perfume bottles," he observes. "The place looked like a charcoal drawing of a town scorched by a dragon."[9]

"I went to the Press House, where journalists were frantically downloading images and writing reports for their agencies. I was sitting with Bilal, the Press House manager, when an explosion shook the building. Windows shattered, and the ceiling collapsed onto us in chunks. We ran toward the central hall. One of the journalists was bleeding, having been hit by flying glass. After twenty minutes, we ventured out to inspect the damage. I noticed that Ramadan decorations were still hanging in the street."[10]

"The city has become a wasteland of rubble and debris," Atef, who was the Palestinian Authority's Minister of Culture, writes in the early days of the Israeli shelling of Gaza City.[11]

"Beautiful buildings fall like columns of smoke. I often think about the time I was shot as a kid, during the first intifada, and how my mother told me I actually died for a few minutes before being brought back to life. Maybe I can do the same this time, I think."[12]

He leaves his teenage son with family members.

"The Palestinian logic is that in wartime, we should all sleep in different places, so that if part of the family is killed, another part lives," he writes. "The UN schools are getting more crowded with displaced families. The hope is that the UN flag will save them, though in previous wars, that hasn't been the case."[13]

On Tuesday, October 17, 2023, he writes:

> I see death approaching, hear its steps growing louder. Just be done with it, I think. It's the eleventh day of the conflict, but all the days have merged into one: the same bombardment, the same fear, the same smell. On the news, I read the names of the dead on the ticker at the bottom of the screen. I wait for my name to appear.
>
> In the morning, my phone rang. It was Rulla, a relative in the West Bank, telling me she had heard there'd been an airstrike in Talat Howa, a neighborhood on the south side of Gaza City where my cousin Hatem lives. Hatem is married to Huda, my wife's only sister. He lives in a four-story building that also houses his mother and brothers and their families.

I called around, but no one's phone was working. I walked to al-Shifa Hospital to read the names: Lists of the dead are pinned up daily outside a makeshift morgue. I could barely approach the building: Thousands of Gazans had made the hospital their home; its gardens, its hallways, every empty space or spare corner had a family in it. I gave up and headed toward Hatem's.

Thirty minutes later, I was on his street. Rulla had been right. Huda and Hatem's building had been hit only an hour earlier. The bodies of their daughter and grandchild had already been retrieved; the only known survivor was Wissam, one of their other daughters, who had been taken to the ICU. Wissam had gone straight into surgery, where both of her legs and her right hand had been amputated. Her graduation ceremony from art college had taken place only the day before. She has to spend the rest of her life without legs, with one hand. "What about the others?" I asked someone.

"We can't find them," came the reply.

Amid the rubble, we shouted: "Hello? Can anyone hear us?" We called out the names of those still missing, hoping some might still be alive. By the end of the day, we'd managed to find five bodies, including that of a three-month-old. We went to the cemetery to bury them.

In the evening, I went to see Wissam in the hospital; she was barely awake. After half an hour, she asked me: "Khalo [Uncle], I'm dreaming, right?"

I said, "We are all in a dream."

"My dream is terrifying! Why?"

"All our dreams are terrifying."

After ten minutes of silence, she said, "Don't lie to me, Khalo. In my dream, I don't have legs. It's true, isn't it? I have no legs?"

"But you said it's a dream."

"I don't like this dream, Khalo."

I had to leave. For a long ten minutes, I cried and cried. Overwhelmed by the horrors of the past few days, I walked out of the hospital and found myself wandering the streets. I thought idly, we could turn this city into a film set for war movies. Second World War films and end-of-the-world movies. We could hire it out to the best Hollywood directors. Doomsday on demand.

Who could have the courage to tell Hanna, so far away in Ramallah, that her only sister had been killed? That her family had been killed? I phoned my colleague Manar and asked her to go to our house with a couple of friends and try to delay the news from getting to her. "Lie to her," I told Manar. "Say the building was attacked by F-16s but the neighbors think Huda and Hatem were out at the time. Any lie that could help."[14]

Leaflets in Arabic dropped by Israeli helicopters float down from the sky. They announce that anyone who remains north of the Wadi waterway will be considered a partner to terrorism, "meaning," Atef writes, "the Israelis can shoot on sight." The electricity is cut. Food, fuel, and water begin to run out.

The wounded are operated on without anesthesia. There are no painkillers or sedatives.[15] He visits his niece Wissam, racked with pain, in Al-Shifa Hospital, who asks him for a lethal injection. She says Allah will forgive her.

"But he will not forgive me, Wissam."

"I am going to ask him to, on your behalf," she says.

After airstrikes, he joins the rescue teams "under the cricket-like hum of drones we couldn't see in the sky." A line from T.S Eliot, "a heap of broken images," runs through his head. The injured and dead are "transported on three-wheeled bicycles or dragged along in carts by animals."

"We picked up pieces of mutilated bodies and gathered them on a blanket; you find a leg here, a hand there, while the rest looks like minced meat," he writes. "In the past week, many Gazans have started writing their names on their hands and legs, in pen or permanent marker, so they can be identified when death comes.

"This might seem macabre," he writes, "but it makes perfect sense: We want to be remembered; we want our stories to be told; we seek dignity. At the very least, our names will be on our graves. The smell of unretrieved bodies under the ruins of a house hit last week remains in the air. The more time passes, the stronger the smell."[16]

The scenes around him become surreal. On November 19, 2023, day forty-four of the assault, he writes:

> A man rides a horse toward me with the body of a dead teenager slung over the saddle in front. It seems it's his son, perhaps. It looks like a scene from a historical movie, only the horse is weak and barely able to move. He is back from no battle. He is no knight. His eyes are full of tears as he holds the little riding crop in one hand and the bridle in the other. I have an impulse to photograph him but then feel suddenly sick at the idea. He salutes no one. He barely looks up. He is too consumed with his own loss. Most people are using the camp's old cemetery; it's the safest and although it is technically long-since full, they have started digging shallower graves and burying the new dead on top of the old—keeping families together, of course.[17]

On November 21, after constant tank shelling, he flees Gaza's Jabaliya neighborhood for the south with his son and seventy-six-year-old mother-in-law, who is in a wheelchair. She will die in February, in a tent in Rafah. They must pass through Israeli checkpoints, where soldiers randomly select men and boys from the line for interrogation and detention.

"Scores of bodies are strewn along both sides of the road," he writes. "Rotting, it seems, into the ground. The smell is horrendous. A hand reaches out toward us from the window of a burned-out car, as if asking for something, from me specifically. I see what looks like two headless bodies in a car—limbs and precious body parts just thrown away and left to fester."

He tells his son Yasser: "Don't look. Just keep walking, son."[18]

In early December Atef's family home is destroyed in an airstrike. He writes:

> The house a writer grows up in is a well from which to draw material. In each of my novels, whenever I wanted to depict a typical house in the camp, I conjured ours. I'd move the furniture around a bit, change the name of the alley, but who was I kidding? It was always our house.
>
> All the houses in Jabaliya are small. They're built randomly, haphazardly, and they're not made to last. These houses replaced the tents that Palestinians like my grandmother Eisha lived in after the displacements of 1948.
>
> Those who built them always thought they'd soon be returning to the beautiful, spacious homes they'd left behind in the towns and villages of historic Palestine. That return never happened, despite our many rituals of hope, like safeguarding the key to the old family home. The future keeps betraying us, but the past is ours.
>
> . . . Though I've lived in many cities around the world, and visited many more, that tiny ramshackle abode was the only place I ever felt at home. Friends and colleagues always asked: Why don't you live in Europe or America? You have the opportunity. My students chimed in: Why did you return to Gaza? My answer was always the same: "Because

in Gaza, in an alleyway in the Saftawi neighborhood of Jab-aliya, there stands a little house that cannot be found any-where else in the world."

If on doomsday God were to ask me where I would like to be sent, I wouldn't hesitate in saying, "Home." Now there is no home.[19]

We turn a corner on a hillside. Cars and trucks veer spas-modically to the right and left. Several in front of us are in reverse. Ahead is an Israeli checkpoint with thick, boxy blocks of dun-colored concrete. Soldiers are stopping vehicles and checking papers. Palestinians can wait hours to get past. They can be hauled from their vehicles and detained. Anything is possible at an Israeli checkpoint, often erected with no advance warning. Most of it is not good.

We back up. We descend a narrow, dusty road that splits off from the main highway. We travel on bumpy, uneven tracks through impoverished villages.

It was like this for Black people in the segregated South and Indigenous Americas. It was like this for Algerians under the French. It was like this in India, Ireland, and Kenya under the British. The death mask of colonialism—too often of European extraction—does not change. Nor does the godlike authority of colonists who look at the colonized as vermin, who take a perverse delight in their humiliation and suffering, and who kill them with impunity.

The Israeli customs official asked me two questions when I crossed into occupied Palestine from Jordan on the King Hussein Bridge.

"Do you hold a Palestinian passport?"

"Are either of your parents Palestinian?"

In short, are you contaminated?

This is how apartheid works.

The Palestinians want their land back. Then they will talk of peace. The Israelis want peace, but demand Palestinian land. And that, in three short sentences, is the intractable nature of this conflict.

I see Jerusalem in the distance. Or rather, I see the Jewish colony that lines the hills above Jerusalem. The villas, built in an arc on the hilltop, have windows intentionally narrowed to upright rectangles to double as gun slits.

We reach the outskirts of Ramallah. We are held up in the snarl of traffic in front of the sprawling Israeli military base that oversees the Qalandia checkpoint, the primary checkpoint between East Jerusalem and the rest of the West Bank. It is the scene of frequent demonstrations against the occupation that can end in gunfire.

I meet Atef. We walk to a kebab shop and sit at a small outdoor table. The scars of the latest incursion by the Israeli army are around the corner. At night, a few days ago, Israeli soldiers torched the shops that handle money transfers from abroad. They are charred ruins. Money from abroad will now be harder to get, which I suspect was the point.

Israel has dramatically tightened its stranglehold on the more than 2.7 million Palestinians in the occupied West Bank, who are surrounded by more than 700,000 Jewish colonists housed in some 150 strategically placed developments with their own shopping malls, schools, and medical centers. These colonial developments, along with special roads that can only be used by the colonists and the military, checkpoints, tracts of land that are off limits to Palestinians, closed military zones, Israeli-declared "nature preserves," and military outposts, form concentric circles. They can instantly sever the flow of traffic to isolate Palestinian cities and towns into a series of ringed ghettos.

"Since October 7, it is hard to travel anywhere in the West Bank," Atef says. "There are checkpoints at the entrances of every city, town, and village. Imagine you want to see your mother or your fiancée. You want to drive from Ramallah to Nablus. It can take seven hours because the main roads are blocked. You are forced to drive through back roads in the mountains."

The trip should take ninety minutes.

It is September 2024. Israeli soldiers and colonists have killed 716 Palestinian civilians, including over 160 children, and injured more than 5,750 others in the West Bank since October 7, according to the Palestinian Health Ministry. Israel has also detained over 9,860 Palestinians—or should I say hostages?—including hundreds of children and pregnant women. Many have been severely tortured, including doctors and paramedics tortured to death in Israeli dungeons and aid workers killed upon their release. Israel's National Security Minister Itamar Ben-Gvir has called for the execution of Palestinian prisoners to free up space for more.

Ramallah, the seat of the Palestinian Authority, was in the past spared the worst of Israeli violence. Since October 7, this has changed. Raids and arrests take place almost daily in and around the city, sometimes accompanied by lethal gunfire and aerial bombardments. Israel has bulldozed or confiscated more than 1,000 Palestinian dwellings and homes in the West Bank since October 7, at times forcing owners to demolish their own buildings or pay exorbitant fines.

Heavily armed Israeli colonists have carried out murderous rampages on villages east of Ramallah, including attacks following the murder of a fourteen-year-old colonist on April 12, 2024, near the village of Al-Mughayyir. The colonists, in retaliation, burned and destroyed Palestinian homes and vehicles across eleven villages, ripped up roads, killed one Palestinian, and wounded more than two dozen others.[20]

"Israel realizes that the world is blind, that no one will force it to end the genocide in Gaza, and no one will pay attention to the war in the West Bank," Atef says. "The word *war* is not even used. This is called a normal Israeli military operation, as if what is happening to us is normal. There is no distinction now between the status of the occupied territories, classified as A, B, and C. The settlers are confiscating more land. They are carrying out more attacks. They do not need the army. They have become a shadow army, supported and armed by Israel's right-wing government. We have lived in a continuous war since 1948. This is simply the newest phase."

Jenin and its neighboring refugee camp are assaulted daily by Israeli armed units, undercover commando teams, and snipers. Drones equipped with machine guns and missiles, as well as warplanes and Apache attack helicopters, circle overhead carrying out targeted assassinations and obliterating dwellings. Armored Caterpillar D9 bulldozers, sometimes fitted with machine guns and grenade launchers, level entire neighborhoods, turning streets and alleys into mounds of broken, jagged concrete. They flatten schools, pharmacies, shops, and houses. They rupture water and sewage pipes, filling streets with fetid pools of raw sewage. Medics and doctors, as in Gaza, are assassinated. Usaid Kamal Jabarin, a fifty-year-old surgeon was killed on May 21, 2024, by an Israel sniper as he arrived for work at the Jenin Governmental Hospital. Hunger is endemic.

"The Israeli military carries out raids that kill Palestinians and then departs," Atef says. "But it returns a few days later. It is not enough for the Israelis to steal our land. They seek to kill as many of the original inhabitants as possible. This is why it carries out constant operations. This is why there are constant armed clashes. But these clashes are provoked by Israel. They are the pretext used to continually attack us. We live under constant pressure. We face death daily."

The dramatic escalation of violence in the West Bank is overshadowed by the genocide in Gaza. But it has become a second front. If Israel can empty Gaza, the West Bank will be next.

"Israel's objective has not changed," he says. "It seeks to shrink the Palestinian population, confiscate larger and larger tracts of Palestinian land, and build more and more colonies. It seeks to Judaize Palestine and strip the Palestinians of all the means to sustain themselves. The ultimate goal is the annexation of the West Bank."

Satellite imagery indicates that the Israeli military has, since October 7, built roads and military bases in over 26 percent of Gaza, suggesting a permanent presence. "Even at the height of the peace process, when everyone was mesmerized by peace, Israel was turning this peace proposal into a nightmare," he goes on. "Most Palestinians were opposed to the peace accords Arafat signed in 1993, but still they welcomed him when he returned. They did not kill him. They wanted to give peace a chance. In Israel, the prime minister who signed the Oslo Accords was assassinated."

Israel has ordered the largest West Bank land seizure in more than three decades, confiscating vast tracts of land northeast of Ramallah. Israel's extreme right-wing Finance Minister Bezalel Smotrich, who lives in a Jewish colony and is in charge of colonial expansion, has promised to flood the West Bank with a million new colonists.[21] He has vowed to obliterate the distinct areas in the West Bank created by the Oslo Accords. In June 2024, Smotrich threatened to annex all of Area A—which comprises eighteen percent of the West Bank and is under exclusive Palestinian control—following the Palestinian Authority's request to the International Criminal Court for arrest warrants for Israeli leaders and for its bid for recognition of a Palestinian state. He also approved the construction of an additional five military outposts. Area B, nearly twenty-two percent of the West Bank, is under Israeli military occupation, in collusion with the Palestinian Authority. Area C, over sixty percent of the West Bank, is under total Israeli occupation.

"A few years ago, someone daubed a strange slogan on the wall of the UN school east of Jabaliya," Atef writes from the hell of

THE OLD EVIL   25

Gaza. "'We progress backwards.' It has a ring to it. Every new war drags us back to basics. It destroys our houses, our institutions, our mosques, and our churches. It razes our gardens and parks. Every war takes years to recover from, and before we've recovered, a new war arrives. There are no warning sirens, no messages sent to our phones. War just arrives."[22]

The Jewish settler-colonial project is protean. It changes its shape but not its essence. Its tactics vary. Its intensity comes in waves of severe repression and less repression. Its rhetoric about peace masks its intent. It grinds forward with deadly, perverted, racist logic. And yet, the Palestinians endure, refusing to submit, resisting despite the overwhelming odds, grasping at tiny kernels of hope from bottomless wells of despair. There is a word for this. Heroic.

II.

# A GENOCIDE FORETOLD

There are no surprises in Gaza. Every horrifying act of Israel's genocide has been telegraphed in advance. It has been for decades. The dispossession of Palestinians of their land is the beating heart of Israel's settler-colonial project. This dispossession has had dramatic historical moments—1948 and 1967—when huge parts of historic Palestine were seized and hundreds of thousands of Palestinians were ethnically cleansed. Dispossession has also occurred in increments—the slow-motion theft of land and steady ethnic cleansing in the West Bank, including East Jerusalem.

I knew Dr. Abdel Aziz Al-Rantisi, the cofounder of Hamas, along with Sheikh Ahmed Ismail Hassan Yassin. Al-Rantisi's family was expelled to the Gaza Strip by Zionist militias from historic Palestine during the 1948 war. He did not fit the demonized image of a Hamas leader. He was a soft-spoken, articulate, and highly educated pediatrician who had graduated first in his class at Egypt's Alexandria University.

As a nine-year-old boy in Khan Yunis, he witnessed the execution of 275 Palestinian men and boys, including his uncle, when Israel briefly occupied the Gaza Strip in 1956, the subject of Joe Sacco's magisterial book *Footnotes in Gaza*. Scores of Palestinians were also executed by Israeli soldiers in the neighboring town of Rafah.

"I still remember the wailing and the tears of my father over his brother," Al-Rantisi said when Joe Sacco and I visited him at his home in Gaza in 2001.

"I couldn't sleep for many months after that . . . It left a wound in my heart that can never heal. I'm telling you a story, and I'm almost crying. This sort of action can never be forgotten . . . They planted hatred in our hearts."[23]

He knew he could never trust the Israelis. He knew that the goal of the Zionist state was the occupation of all of historic Palestine—Israel seized Gaza and the West Bank in 1967 along with Syria's Golan Heights and Egypt's Sinai Peninsula—and the eternal subjugation or extermination of the Palestinian people. He knew he would avenge the killings.

Al-Rantisi and Yassin were assassinated by Israel in 2004. Al-Rantisi's widow, Jamila Abdallah Taha Al-Shanti, had a doctorate in English and taught at the Islamic University in Gaza. The couple had six children, one of whom was killed along with his father. The family's home was bombed and destroyed during the 2014 Israeli assault on Gaza known as Operation Protective Edge. Jamila was killed by Israel on October 19, 2023.

Hamas, like all resistance groups, from the African National Congress to the Irish Republican Army, is as demonized as it is misunderstood. Hamas is a religious, nationalist liberation movement. While it has carried out indiscriminate suicide bombings against Israeli civilians, while its incursion into Israel on October 7 included atrocities, and while its 1988 founding charter calls for Israel's destruction, Hamas is not, despite what Israel and Washington say, a terrorist organization. Hamas was founded as a civil society and political movement during the First Intifada in 1987. It didn't establish its military wing—the Qassam Brigades—until 1992. It gained widespread support among Palestinians in Gaza by establishing schools, summer camps, food banks, and medical clinics.

Like most armed resistance groups—including the Jewish militias that created the state of Israel—it uses terrorism as a tactic.

And Hamas has proven to be flexible, including an acceptance in 2017 of a two-state solution along with numerous negotiations with Israel facilitated by Egyptian and Qatari interlocutors. Hamas does not hold the Palestinians in Gaza hostage. It has popular support among Palestinians, largely because of the failure of the Palestine Liberation Organization (PLO) to deliver on the promises made by Israel in the 1993 Oslo Accords. Rather than abide by the Oslo Accords, which were supposed to lead to a two-state solution, Israel increased its colonies in the West Bank from 128 to 371. The numbers of Jewish settlers have grown from around 250,000 to more than 700,000. Israel passed the 2018 Nation State Law that asserts exclusive Jewish sovereignty over "Eretz Yisrael." It calls Jewish settlement on occupied Palestinian land a "national priority." Israel dismisses Palestinian assertions of self-determination as a security threat and uses such assertions to legitimize permanent occupation.

But Hamas also has popular support because of its dogged resistance to Israel's attacks on Gaza. Indeed, since the genocide, Hamas has become lionized throughout the Muslim world.

The secular Palestinian Authority, which nominally governs the occupied West Bank, is a hated colonial police force. It has failed to blunt Israel's slow-motion ethnic cleansing, proved powerless to halt the eviction of Palestinians from their homes and land in the West Bank, including East Jerusalem, and is unable to thwart Israeli raids, incursions, deadly shootings, and the seizing of water resources. It also, on Israel's behalf as well as its own, prohibits demonstrations and protests and works in coordination with Israeli intelligence services to hunt down Hamas militants.[24]

Israel rears successive generations of enraged, traumatized, and dispossessed Palestinians who have lost family members, friends, homes, communities, and any hope of living ordinary lives.

They hate as they have been hated. This lust for vengeance is universal. After World War II, a clandestine unit of Jews who served in the Jewish Brigade of the British Army called "Gmul"—Hebrew for "Recompense"—hunted down former Nazis and executed them.

As W.H. Auden writes:

> *I and the public know*
> *What all schoolchildren learn,*
> *Those to whom evil is done*
> *Do evil in return.*[25]

Chaim Engel, who took part in the uprising at the Nazis' Sobibor death camp in Poland, described how, armed with a knife, he attacked a guard in the camp.

"It's not a decision," Engel said. "You just react, instinctively you react to that, and I figured, 'Let us to do, and go and do it.' And I went. I went with the man in the office, and we killed this German. With every jab, I said, 'That is for my father, for my mother, for all these people, all the Jews you killed."[26]

What Engel did to the Nazi guard was no less savage than what Hamas and other resistance fighters did to Israelis in October 2023, after escaping their own prison. Taken out of context, it is inexplicable. But set against the backdrop of the extermination camp, or the seventeen years trapped in Gaza's concentration camp, it makes sense.

This is not to excuse it. To understand is not to condone. But we *must* understand if this cycle of violence is to be stopped. No one is immune to the thirst for vengeance.

J. Glenn Gray, a combat officer in World War II, writes about the peculiar nature of vengeance in *The Warriors: Reflections on Men in Battle*:

> When the soldier has lost a comrade to this enemy or possibly had his family destroyed by them through bombings or through political atrocities, so frequently the case in World

War II, his anger and resentment deepen into hatred. Then the war for him takes on the character of a vendetta. Until he has himself destroyed as many of the enemy as possible, his lust for vengeance can hardly be appeased.

I have known soldiers who were avid to exterminate every last one of the enemy, so fierce was their hatred. Such soldiers took great delight in hearing or reading of mass destruction through bombings. Anyone who has known or been a soldier of this kind is aware of how hatred penetrates every fiber of his being. His reason for living is to seek revenge; not an eye for an eye and a tooth for a tooth, but a tenfold retaliation.[27]

The Palestinian attacks of October 7 feed this lust within Israel, just as Israel's obliteration of Gaza feeds this lust among Palestinians. Israel's blue and white national flag with the Star of David adorns homes and cars. Crowds gather to support families whose members are among the hostages in Gaza. Israelis hand out food at road junctions to soldiers headed to Gaza. Banners with slogans such as "Israel at war" and "Together we will win" punctuate television broadcasts and media sites. There has been little discussion in Israeli media of the slaughter in Gaza or the suffering of Palestinians—nearly all of whom have been driven from their homes—but a constant repetition of the stories of suffering, death, and heroism that took place during the October 7 attack. *Only our victims matter.*

"Few of us ever know how far fear and violence can transform us into creatures at bay, ready with tooth and claw," Gray wrote. "If the war taught me anything at all, it convinced me that people are not what they seem or even think themselves to be."[28]

Marguerite Duras, in her book *The War: A Memoir*, writes of how she and other members of the French Resistance tortured a fifty-year-old Frenchman accused of collaborating with the Nazis.

Two men who were tortured in Montluc Prison in Lyon strip the alleged informer. They beat him as the group shouts: "Bastard. Traitor. Scum." Blood and mucus soon run from his nose. His eye is damaged. He moans, "Ow, ow, oh, oh." He crumples in a heap on the floor. Duras writes that he had "become someone without anything in common with other men. And with every minute the difference grows bigger and more established." She watches the beating passively. "The more they hit and the more he bleeds, the more it's clear that hitting is necessary, right, just." She goes on: "You have to strike. There will never be any justice in the world unless you—yourself are justice now. Judges, paneled courtrooms play-acting, not justice." She notes, "Every blow rings out in the silent room. They're hitting at all the traitors, at the women who left, at all those who didn't like what they saw from behind the shutters."[29]

Zionism is the engine behind a century of Palestinian and Arab rage. The Palestinian resistance has little more than small arms and rocket-propelled grenades to battle against one of the best-equipped and most technologically advanced militaries on the planet. Israel may be able to hunt down and kill Hamas leaders—including the chairman of Hamas's Political Bureau, Ismail Haniyeh, who was assassinated in July 2024 during a visit to Tehran—but it makes no difference. Resistance movements are built on the blood of martyrs. Israel ensures a continual supply.

The start of Operation Al-Aqsa Flood on October 7, 2023, was accompanied by a deluge of Israeli propaganda. Claims of beheaded babies, infants burned alive in ovens, mass rape, and other heinous atrocities allegedly committed by Hamas were disseminated by Israel and promoted by a range of interlocutors that included journalists, celebrities, legacy media, and the Biden administration.

There's growing evidence that in the chaotic fighting that took place once Hamas militants entered Israel, the Israeli military targeted not only Hamas fighters, but Israeli captives with them.[30]

Tuval Escapa, a member of the security team for Kibbutz Be'eri, told the Israeli press he set up a hotline to coordinate between kibbutz residents and the Israeli army. "The commanders in the field made difficult decisions, including shelling houses on their occupants in order to eliminate the terrorists along with the hostages," he told the newspaper *Haaretz*.[31]

The newspaper reported that Israeli commanders were "compelled to request an aerial strike against its own facility inside the Erez Crossing to Gaza in order to repulse the terrorists who had seized control."[32] That base housed Israeli Civil Administration officers and soldiers.

Israel, in 1986, instituted a military policy called the Hannibal Directive—apparently named after the Carthaginian general who poisoned himself rather than be captured by the Romans—following the capture of two Israeli soldiers by Hezbollah.[33] The Directive is designed to prevent Israeli troops from falling into enemy hands through the maximum use of force, even at the cost of killing the captured soldiers and civilians. The Directive was executed during the 2014 Israeli assault on Gaza, known as Operation Protective Edge. Hamas fighters on August 1, 2014, captured an Israeli soldier, Lieutenant Hadar Goldin. In response, Israel dropped more than two thousand bombs, missiles, and shells on the area where he was being held. Goldin was killed along with over one hundred Palestinian civilians.[34] The directive was supposedly rescinded in 2016.

Israel is granted impunity from its violations of international law, occupation of Palestinian land, and genocide in Gaza because it has built a lobby with staggering financial resources and a well-oiled machine that props up politicians that support the apartheid state while aggressively funding campaigns to unseat politicians that defend Palestinian rights.

The list of politicians torpedoed by the Israel lobby includes Arkansas Senator J. William Fulbright, who, as chairman of the

Senate Foreign Relations Committee, issued a three-hundred-page report that revealed "various pro-Zionist organizations used tax-free United Jewish Appeal money, meant to help poor communities in Israel, in order to fund [American Israel Public Affairs Committee] AIPAC's activities in the USA."[35]

"The campaign against him became a model," Israeli historian Ilan Pappé writes. "*The Near East Report* accused him of being 'consistently unkind to Israel and our supporters in this country.' Everything was done to ensure that he would not be reelected. Lobby money poured into the campaign coffers of his rival, Arkansas Governor Dale Bumpers, in the May 1974 Democratic primary election. Anyone standing against him was financed and supported."[36]

As Pappé notes, "AIPAC manipulated Congress policy with such successful results that very few have since dared to follow in Fulbright's footsteps."[37]

The latest Democratic Party casualties are Rep. Cori Bush, who lost her primary in Missouri in August 2024, and Rep. Jamaal Bowman from New York, who lost his primary in June 2024. AIPAC and the United Democracy Project, AIPAC's super PAC, spent more than $8 million to defeat Bush and over $15 million in the most expensive primary race in US history to defeat Bowman.[38] Bush and Bowman called for a halt to the genocide. *Politico* reported that AIPAC was planning on spending $100 million on the 2024 elections.[39]

*The Lobby—USA*, a four-part *Al Jazeera* documentary about the Israel lobby in the United States, was blocked under heavy Israeli pressure shortly before its release. A leaked copy was posted online by the Chicago-based news outlet *The Electronic Intifada*, the French website *Orient XXI*, and the Lebanese newspaper *Al-Akhbar*.[40]

The series is an inside look over five months by an undercover reporter, armed with a hidden camera, at how the government and intelligence agencies of Israel work with US domestic Jewish lobby groups such as AIPAC, The Israel Project, and Stand-WithUs, to spy on, smear, and attack critics, especially American university students who support the Boycott, Divestment, and Sanctions (BDS) movement. It shows how the Israel lobby uses huge cash donations, often far above the US legal limit and flies hundreds of members of Congress to Israel for lavish vacations at Israeli seaside resorts, bribing the American lawmakers to do Israel's bidding, including providing military aid such as the $38 billion (over ten years) that was approved by Congress in 2016.[41] The documentary uncovers the lobby's slandering and character assassination of academics, activists, and journalists, its well-funded fake grassroots activism, its manipulation of press coverage, and its ham-fisted attempts to destroy marriages, personal relationships, and careers.

The series highlights the efforts to discredit liberal Jews and Jewish organizations as tools of radical jihadists, referring, for example, to Jewish Voice for Peace as "Jewish Voice for Hamas," and claims that many members of the organization are not actually Jewish. Israel recruits Black South Africans into an Israeli front group called Stop Stealing My Apartheid in a desperate effort to counter the reality of the apartheid state Israel has constructed. The series documents Israel's repeated and multifaceted interference in the internal affairs of the United States, including elections; efforts to discredit progressive groups such as Black Lives Matter that express sympathy for Palestinians; and routine employment of Americans to spy on other Americans. Israel's behavior is unethical and perhaps illegal. But don't expect anyone in the establishment or either of the two ruling parties to do anything about it. It is abundantly clear by the end of the series that they have been intimidated, discredited, or bought off.

"Imagine if China was doing this, if Iran was doing this, if Russia was doing this?" Ali Abunimah, author of *The Battle for Justice in Palestine* and cofounder of *The Electronic Intifada*, says in the film. "There would be uproar. You would have Congress going after them. You would have hearings."

The power of *The Lobby—USA* is that in dealing with the undercover reporter—a young Oxford postgraduate, James Anthony Kleinfeld, who goes by the name Tony and poses as a pro-Israel student—major figures within the Israel lobby candidly explain how they operate. There is no plausible deniability. And this is why the exposé was never broadcasted.

Clayton Swisher, who directed the series, wrote in the liberal Jewish newspaper *The Forward* that leaders from the Israel lobby met with the state of Qatar's registered agent and lobbyist, a former aide to US Senator Ted Cruz named Nick Muzin, to "see if he could use his ties with the Qataris to stop the airing."[42] *Al Jazeera* is primarily funded by the Qatari government.[43] Muzin told the Israeli newspaper *Haaretz* that "he was discussing the issue with the Qataris and didn't think the film would broadcast in the near future." An anonymous source told *Haaretz* that "the Qatari emir himself helped make the decision" to spike the series.[44]

Saudi Arabia, Egypt, Bahrain, and the United Arab Emirates severed ties with Qatar in June 2017 and imposed a land, sea, and air blockade on the Persian Gulf state. They accused Doha of supporting terrorism and radical Islamist groups, including the Muslim Brotherhood. The four states issued a list of demands for reestablishing ties that included Qatar's shutting down of *Al Jazeera*, along with severing relations with Iran. Qatar appealed to the United States to intercede and, as part of this effort, reached out to the Israel lobby in the US for support. American Jewish leaders, including the former Harvard law professor Alan Dershowitz, met with the Qatari emir, Tamim bin Hamad Al Thani, and discussed what they described as the network's "anti-Semitism." It is widely believed the series was sacrificed by Qatar in an effort to placate the Israel lobby and get its support for an end to Saudi Arabia's sanctions, which they lifted in 2021.

Israeli intelligence services, the series reveals, monitor American critics of Israel and feed real-time information about them to American Jewish organizations.

"We are, for example, in the process of creating a comprehensive picture of the campuses," Brigadier General Sima Vaknin-Gil, director general of Israel's Ministry of Strategic Affairs, tells a gathering of pro-Israel activists in the film. "If you want to defeat a phenomenon you must have the upper hand in terms of information and knowledge."

The Israeli government operates Israel Cyber Shield, a civil intelligence unit that collects and analyzes boycott and divestment activities and coordinates attacks against the BDS movement.

"We are giving them data—for example, one day Sima's deputy is sending me a photo. Just a photo on WhatsApp," Sagi Balasha, who was CEO of the Israeli-American Council from 2011 to 2015, says when speaking on an Israeli-American Council panel. "It's written 'Boycott Israel' on the billboard."

He shows a picture of a roadside billboard that reads: "boycott israel until palestinians have equal rights. StopFundingApartheid.org."

"In a few hours our systems and analysts could find the exact organization, people, and even their names, and where they live," says Balasha, who works with cyber intelligence organizations that target BDS activists. "We gave it back to the ministry, and I have no idea what they did with this. But the fact is, three days later there were no billboards."

"We use all sorts of technology," Jacob Baime, the executive director of the Israel on Campus Coalition, says in the film. "We use corporate-level, enterprise-grade social media intelligence software. Almost all of this happens on social media, so we have custom algorithms and formulae that acquire this stuff immediately."

"Generally, within about thirty seconds or less of one of these things popping up on campus, whether it's a Facebook event, whether it's the right kind of mention on Twitter, the system picks it up," says Baime. "It goes into a queue and alerts our researchers and they evaluate it. They tag it, and if it rises to a certain level, we issue early-warning alerts to our partners."

Those recruited by the Israel lobby, including the undercover *Al Jazeera* reporter in the documentary, are sent to training sessions such as Fuel For Truth. The film records a session in which trainees watch a video of Palestinian children as the narrator says, "Children are taught in UNRWA [United Nations Relief and Works Agency for Palestine Refugees in the Near East] Palestinian schools to hate Jews." The trainees are told that scenes of devastation in Gaza are, in fact, misrepresented images disseminated by critics from Syria or Iraq. They are instructed in role-playing workshops how to brand all those who criticize Israeli policies as anti-Semites, members of a hate group, or self-hating Jews.

The reporter is placed in the so-called "war room" run by The Israel Project, known as TIP, which monitors American media for stories on Israel and the Palestinians. The goal is "neutralizing undesired narratives."

"We develop relationships," David Hazony, managing director of The Israel Project, says about how to influence journalists. "A lot of alcohol to get them to trust us. We're basically messaging on the following: BDS is essentially a kind of a hate group targeting Israel. They're anti-peace. We try not to even use the terms because it builds their brand. We just refer to boycotters. The goal is to actually make things happen. And to figure out what are the means of communication to do that."

The Boycott, Divestment, Sanctions movement was formed in 2005. It is an attempt by Palestinian civil rights groups to build a nonviolent international movement to boycott Israel, divest from Israeli companies, and eventually impose sanctions—as was done against apartheid South Africa—until basic Palestinian rights under international law are achieved. While the movement has gained little traction financially in the United States, with most colleges and universities refusing to divest, it has been very effective at illuminating the injustices committed against Palestinians by Israel and severely eroded Israel's credibility and support. Israel and its lobby have poured millions of dollars into crushing the movement. The core demands of BDS were adopted by many of the encampments on university campuses erected to protest the genocide in 2024.

"Government ministers attacked me in person," Omar Barghouti, cofounder of the BDS movement, says in the documentary. "One of them threatened BDS leaders with targeted civil assassination. Others threatened to revoke my permanent residency [in Israel], along with other threats."

"We suffered from intense denial-of-service attacks, hacking attacks on our website," Barghouti says. "Israel decided to go on cyber warfare against BDS. Publicly, they said, 'We shall spy on BDS individuals and networks, especially in the West.' We have not heard a peep from any Western government complaining that Israel is admitting that it will spy on your citizens. Imagine Iran saying it will spy on British or American citizens. Just imagine what could happen."

"So, like nobody really knows what we're doing," says Julia Reifkind, who was Director of Community Affairs at the Israeli Embassy in Washington, in the documentary. "But mainly it's been a lot of research, like monitoring BDS things and reporting it back to the Ministry of Foreign Affairs. Like making sure everyone knows what's going on. They need a lot of research done and stuff like that. When they talk about it in the Knesset, we've usually contributed to what the background information is. I'm not going to campuses. It's more about connecting organizations and I guess campuses, providing resources and strategy if students need it.

"I write a report and give it to my boss, who translates it," Reifkind says. "It's really weird. We don't talk to them on the phone or email. There's a special server that's really secure that I don't have access to because I'm an American. You have to have clearance to access the server. It's called Cables. It's not even the same [word translated] in Hebrew, it's like literally 'Cables.' I've seen it. It looks really bizarre. So, I write reports that my boss translates into the Cables and sends them. Then they'll send something back. Then he'll translate it and tell me what I need to do."

"Is the Israeli Embassy trying to leverage faculty?" Tony, the undercover reporter, asks her.

"Yeah," she says. "We are working with several faculty advocacy groups that kind of train faculty, and so we are helping them a little bit with funding, connections, bringing them to speak, having them to speak to diplomats and people at the MFA [Ministry of Foreign Affairs] that need this information. So, I want to be that resource to show students what we're doing, to see what you're doing, here's some information if you need anything at all. We can connect you. Just kind of be that person there for you."

Reifkind was president of the pro-Israel group at the University of California at Davis and worked closely with the Israel lobby to attempt to crush the BDS movement on campus, especially after Students for Justice in Palestine (SJP) brought a divestment motion to the student senate.

"We knew they were going to win because the entire student senate was all pro-BDS," she says. "They ran for that purpose and won for that purpose. We have been pushed out of student government for months."

Reifkind and a few supporters went to the senate meeting where the vote was scheduled.

"We have been ignored and disrespected year after year, but we have never been silenced," she tells the student gathering. "We are a beacon of peace and inclusion on a campus plagued by anti-Semitism."

"The intolerance that spawned this [divestment] resolution is the same kind of intolerance that spawned anti-Semitic movements throughout history," she shouts.

She and her handful of supporters walk out, an action they had agreed on in advance and then carefully filmed.

The passing of the BDS motion at UC Davis set the gears of the Israel lobby and the Israeli government in motion.

"That day all of us released like fifty op-eds in major news sources so that when people made a hashtag, like a whole thing trending, so when people opened their Facebooks it wouldn't be them celebrating their victory," Reifkind says in the film. "It would be us sharing our stories. Once it blew up, then random people like *The Huffington Post* contacted me and was like, 'Do you have anything to say?' And I was like, 'Conveniently, I wrote an op-ed two weeks ago just in case.'"

Israel and its surrogates carried out vicious and anonymous personal attacks against the campus BDS activists at UC Davis, calling them "terrorists" and "Hamas sympathizers" who support the imposition of Sharia—Islamic law—on campus. The lobby also framed the narrative in the national media, claiming falsely that the pro-Israel students were forced out of the meeting room. These tactics would become very familiar to the students in the encampments protesting the genocide.

"Pro-Israel students were taunted by pro-Hamas students after an anti-Israel vote passed on campus," says an announcer on *Fox News* as a caption underneath the video reads, "RUNNING RAMPANT: UC Davis Plagued by Anti-Semitic Feelings." "And right after the vote passed, a student senator posted this on Facebook, 'Hamas and Sharia law have taken over UC Davis. Brb [be right back] crying over the resilience.'"

Shortly after the vote, Jewish students said they found two swastikas painted on their fraternity house in Davis. The media, tipped off, was at the fraternity house almost immediately. The BDS activists were blamed for the graffiti.

The film shows a *CBS 13* news clip.

Television reporter: "Pro-Israel students said they feared recent events would lead to this."

UC Davis male student: "This has been sort of a bad week to be Jewish on campus."

Television reporter: "After years of heated meetings, the student body passed a resolution Thursday, urging UC Davis to end any affiliation with companies that support Israel."

Another UC Davis male student, speaking in front of one of the swastikas: "So, this is not out of the blue. We're pretty sure this is directly related."

"StandWithUs helped us a little bit in terms of actual research on the speech," Reifkind says when referring to her comments before the student senate. "They gave us some legal research-type stuff. I'm always biased and want to work with AIPAC. They kind of helped, more like moral support. And David Project helped us a little bit. It was more help like gaining contacts in the media world. I guess we needed money to pay for someone to film the speech. We had a Davis Faculty for Israel group, and they were hugely helpful to us. Some of them were retired lawyers, they'd write legal documents for us. They knew the administration. They were tenured. They had pull."

"After looking back on everything, I feel a little creepy because of what happened after the vote," says Marcelle Obeid, the president of Students for Justice in Palestine at UC Davis. "People who were affiliated with the [pro-Palestinian] group were just smeared and had to deal with these very personal crises—the world calling us 'terrorists,' the world thinking that we were this spiteful hate group. It's pretty unequivocal how organized they were, how brutal and ruthless that narrative was, and how it affected us."

*The Electronic Intifada's* Abunimah says, "There's an intensive effort by Israel and pro-Israel groups to get governments, universities, legislative bodies to adopt a definition of anti-Semitism that includes criticism of Israel and its state ideology, Zionism."

"They have created this perverse definition of anti-Semitism where calling for everyone in Palestine and Israel to have equal rights is somehow an attack on Jews," he says. "They're trying to get this pushed into official definitions. This has been a key goal of the Brandeis Center so they can go after people who are advocating for equality and bring them up on charges that they're actually anti-Semitic bigots."

Kenneth Marcus, founding president of the Louis D. Brandeis Center for Human Rights Under Law, confirms this stance in the film, saying: "You have to show that they're racist hate groups, that they are using intimidation to get funded, and to consistently portray them that way."

But despite its campaign, Israel is acutely aware that it is losing the public relations war, especially among the young.

"The polling isn't good," David Brog, executive director of the Maccabee Task Force, which combats BDS on American campuses, says in the film. "And all of you probably know that if you look at the polls, the younger you get on the demographic scales, the lower support for Israel is . . . it seems to be achieving its goals. I think it threatens future American support for Israel. Younger people are leaving college less sympathetic to Israel than when they entered."

And many of these young people are Jewish, finding their identity and meaning in values that Israel refuses to uphold.

"The work that Jewish Voice for Peace does is grounded in Jewish tradition, the most basic Jewish and human values that every single person has inherent worth and dignity and should be treated with respect," Rabbi Joseph Berman says in the film. "We then see what's happening to Palestinians, the occupation, the displacement, the inequality, and say we need to end these things."

But while Israel may be losing in the court of public opinion, it continues to control elected officials in the United States, where legalized bribery is institutionalized.

"Does the war of ideas matter?" asks Eric Gallagher, who was a director of AIPAC from 2010 to 2015. "I don't know. I don't know.

I know that getting $38 billion in security aid to Israel matters, which is what AIPAC just did. That's what I'm proud to have been a part of for so long. My job was basically to convince students that participating in the war of ideas on campuses is actually a distraction. You can hold up signs and have rallies on campus, but the Congress gets $3.1 billion a year for Israel. Everything AIPAC does is focused on influencing Congress. Congress is where you have leverage. So, you can't influence the President of the United States directly, but the Congress can."

"What the lobby is all about is to make sure that Israel gets special treatment from the United States, forever," John Mearsheimer, professor of political science at the University of Chicago and coauthor of *The Israel Lobby and US Foreign Policy*, says in the film. "What AIPAC does is it makes sure that money is funneled your way if you're seen as pro-Israel, and it will go to significant lengths to make sure that you stay in office if you continue to be staunchly pro-Israel."

"What happens is Jeff [Talpins] meets with congressmen in the backroom, tells them exactly what his goals are," David Ochs, founder of HaLev says of the pro-Israeli hedge fund manager, and how politicians receive sums of as much as $200,000 from the Israel lobby. "And by the way, Jeff Talpins is worth $250 million. Basically, they hand an envelope with twenty credit cards and say, 'You can swipe each of these credit cards for $1,000 each.'"

"If you wander off the reservation and become critical of Israel, you not only will not get money, AIPAC will go to great lengths to find someone who will run against you, and support that person very generously," Mearsheimer says. "The end result is you're likely to lose your seat in Congress."

"They have questionnaires," recalls former US Rep. Jim Moran, a Democrat from northern Virginia who was in the House from 1991 to 2015. Moran, who opposed the 2002 congressional resolution to invade Iraq, became a target for the Israel lobby, which pushed hard for the war. "Anyone running for Congress is required [by the lobby] to fill out a questionnaire. And they [AIPAC] evaluate the depth of your commitment to Israel on the basis of that question-naire. And then you have an interview with local people. If you get AIPAC support, then more often than not you're going to win.

"There was a conservative rabbi in my district who was assigned to me, I assume, by AIPAC," Moran says. "He warned me that if I voiced my views about the Israeli lobby that my career would be over, and implied that it would be done through *The* [*Washington*] *Post*. Sure enough, *The Washington Post* editorialized bru-tally. Everyone ganged up."

Character assassination is a common tactic used by the Israel lobby against its critics. Bill Mullen, a professor of American studies at Purdue University, has been a campaigner for the BDS movement for years. His wife was sent a link to a website con-taining a letter addressed to her.

"It was a Sunday," he says. "I was in the kitchen. My partner was in the living room with my daughter. She came in with her laptop and said, 'You've got to see this.' This letter, reported to be by a former student, said she had been sexually harassed by me. She had found other students at Purdue who have had the same expe-rience. And she was writing this letter to tell their story. Within a very short time, within about forty-eight hours, we were able to establish that these multiple sites that were attacking me had been taken out [created] almost at the same time. And that they were clearly the work of the same people. One of the accounts said, in the process of supposedly putting my hand on her, I invited her to a Palestine organizational meeting. Well, I thought, 'You're sort of putting your cards on the table there, whoever you are.'"

"With the anti-Israel people, what we found has been most effective, in the last year, you do the opposition research," says Baime, the Israel on Campus Coalition official. "Put up an anon-ymous website. Then put up targeted Facebook ads. Every few hours you drip out a new piece of opposition research, it's psychological warfare. It drives them crazy. They either shut down or they spend time investigating it and responding to it, which is time they can't spend attacking Israel. That's incredibly effective."

"It was really an attempt, by people who didn't know us, 'Maybe I can destroy this marriage at the very least,'" Purdue's Mullen says. "'Maybe I can cause them horrendous, personal suffering.' The same letter purporting to be harassment, sent to my wife, used the name of our daughter. I think that was the worst moment. We thought, 'These people will do anything. They're capable of doing anything.'"

Perhaps the documentary's greatest investigative coup is the unwitting disclosure by Eric Gallagher of The Israel Project that the hedge fund manager Adam Milstein is "the guy who funds" the anonymous Canary Mission website. The website provides the names, backgrounds, and photos of students, professors, invited speakers, and organizations and smears them as being tied to terrorism and anti-Semitism because of their support for Palestinian rights.

"There's a guy named Adam Milstein who you might want to meet," Gallagher says to Tony, the undercover reporter. "He's a convicted felon. That's a bad way to describe him. He's a real estate mogul. When I was working with him at AIPAC, I was literally emailing back and forth with him while he was in jail. He's loaded. He's close to half a billion dollars."

Milstein was convicted of tax evasion and sent to prison for three months in 2009. The Israeli-American Council, which he leads, funds numerous pro-Israel organizations: Milstein also sits on the boards of AIPAC, StandWithUs, and the Israel on Campus Coalition. He was close to billionaire casino magnate Sheldon Adelson—who died in 2021—the wealthiest donor to the pro-Israel lobby and the largest donor to Trump's 2016 election campaign. Adelson's widow, Miriam, made a $100-million pledge in 2024 to fund the pro-Trump Preserve America super PAC.[45]

The promotional video for the Canary Mission, played in the documentary, says: "A few years later, these individuals are applying for jobs in your companies . . . ensure that today's radicals are not tomorrow's employees."

"It was shattering to me because I had to look for a job, I had to start my life," Obeid from UC Davis says. "And now I had this website smearing my name before I even got a chance to make a name for myself."

"Somebody did contact my employer and asked for me to be fired based on my pro-Palestine activism," says Summer Award, who campaigned at the University of Tennessee for Palestinian rights. "They said if they continued to employ me, their values are anti-Semitic. It can be really scary at first. I was mostly harassed via Twitter. They were tweeting me every two or three days. They take screenshots, even way back to my Facebook pictures that don't even look like me anymore. Just digging and digging through my online presence."

Tony joins an astroturf protest organized by the Hoover Institution. Those in the protest have been paid to travel on a bus to George Mason University to disrupt a conference of SJP. They are coached by Yael Lerman Mazar, the StandWithUs director of legal affairs, on what to shout.

"If you do happen to speak with any reporters just stay on message," Mazar tells her lackluster protesters. "And what is the message? SJP is a . . ."

"Hate group," the protesters answer feebly.

III.

# THE DEATH OF AMR

On the morning Amr Abdallah was killed, he woke before dawn to say his Ramadan prayers with his father, mother, two younger brothers, and aunt, in an open field in southern Gaza.

"It is You we worship and You we ask for help," they prayed. "Guide us to the straight path—the path of those upon whom You have bestowed favor, not of those who have evoked Your anger or of those who are astray."

It was dark. They made their way back to their tents. Their old life was gone—their village, Al-Qarara, their house built with the money Amr's father saved during the thirty years he worked in the Persian Gulf—their orchards, their school, the local mosque, and the town's cultural museum with artifacts dating from 4,000 B.C.[46]

Blasted into rubble.[47]

Amr, who was seventeen, would have graduated from high school in 2024, but the schools were shut down in November 2023.[48] He would have gone to college, perhaps to be an engineer like his father, who was a prominent community leader. Amr was a gifted student. Now he lived in a tent in a designated "safe area," which Israel sporadically shelled.

It was cold and rainy. The family huddled together to keep warm. Hunger wrapped itself around them like a coil.

"When you say 'Amr' it's like you're talking about the moon," his uncle, Abdulbaset Abdallah, who lives in New Jersey, tells me. "He was the special one—handsome, brilliant, and kind."

The Israeli attacks began in northern Gaza. Then they spread south. On the morning of Friday, December 1, 2023, Israeli drones dropped leaflets over Amr's village.

"To the inhabitants of Al-Qarara, Khirbet Khaza'a, Abasan and Bani Suheila," the leaflets read. "You must evacuate immediately and go to shelters in the Rafah area. The city of Khan Yunis is a dangerous combat zone. You have been warned. Signed by the Israeli Defense Army."

Families in Gaza live together. Whole generations. This is why dozens of family members are killed in a single airstrike. Amr grew up surrounded by uncles, aunts, and cousins.

The villagers panicked. Some began to pack. Some refused to leave.

One of Amr's uncles was adamant. He would stay behind while the family would go to the "safe area." His son was a physician at Nasser Hospital. Amr's cousin left the hospital to plead with his father to leave. Moments after he and his father fled, their street was bombed.

Amr and his family moved in with relatives in Khan Yunis. A few days later, more leaflets were dropped. Everyone was told to go to Rafah.

Amr's family, now joined by relatives from Khan Yunis, fled to Rafah.[49]

Rafah was a nightmare. Desperate Palestinians were living in the open air and on the streets. There was little food or water. The family slept in their car. It was cold and rainy. They did not have blankets. They looked desperately for a tent. There were no tents. They found an old sheet of plastic, which they attached to the back of the car to make a protected area. There were no bathrooms. People relieved themselves on the side of the road. The stench was overpowering.

They had been displaced twice in the span of a week.

Amr's father, who has diabetes and high blood pressure, fell sick. The family took him to the European Hospital near Khan Yunis. The doctor told him he was ill because he was not eating enough.

"We can't handle your case," the doctor told him. "There are more critical cases."

"He had a beautiful house," Abdallah says of his older brother. "Now he is homeless. He knew everyone in his hometown. Now he lives on the street with crowds of strangers. No one has enough to eat. There is no clean water. There are no proper facilities or bathrooms."

The family decided to move again to Al-Mawasi, designated a "humanitarian area" by Israel.[50] They would at least be in open land, some of which belonged to their family. The coastal area, filled with dunes, became a refuge for hundreds of thousands of displaced Palestinians. The Israelis promised the delivery of international humanitarian aid to Al-Mawasi, little of which arrived.[51] Water was trucked in. There was no electricity.

Israeli warplanes hit a residential compound in Al-Mawasi in January 2024, where medical teams and their families from the International Rescue Committee and Medical Aid for Palestinians were housed.[52] Several were injured. An Israeli tank fired on a house in Al-Mawasi where staff from Médecins Sans Frontières and their families were sheltering in February, killing two and injuring six.[53]

Amr's family set up two makeshift tents with palm tree leaves and sheets of plastic. Israeli drones circled overhead night and day.

On the day before he was killed, Amr managed to get a phone connection to speak to his sister in Canada.

"Please get us out of here," he pleaded.

The Egyptian firm Hala, which means "Welcome" in Arabic, provided travel permits for Gazans to enter Egypt for $350 before the Israeli assault. Since the genocide began, the firm has raised the price to $5,000 for an adult and $2,500 for a child.[54] It has sometimes charged as much as $10,000 for a travel permit since October 7, 2023.

Hala has offices in Cairo and Rafah. Once the money is paid—Hala only accepts US dollars—the name of the applicant is submitted to Egyptian authorities. It can take weeks to get a permit. It would cost around $25,000 to get Amr's family out of Gaza, double that if they included his widowed aunt and three cousins. This was not a sum Amr's relatives abroad could raise quickly.

Once Palestinians get to Egypt, the permits expire within forty-five days. Most of the Palestinian refugees in Egypt survive on money sent to them from abroad. There are some 100,000 Palestinians from Gaza in Egypt, and most live in destitution.

Amr awoke in the dark. It was the first Friday of Ramadan. He joined his family in the morning prayer. The Fajr. It was five a.m.

Muslims fast in the day during the month of Ramadan. They eat and drink once the sun goes down and shortly before dawn. But food was now in very short supply. A little olive oil. The spice za'atar. It was not much.

They went back to their tents after prayers. Amr was in the tent with his aunt and three cousins. A shell exploded nearby. Shrapnel tore apart his aunt's leg and critically injured his cousins. Amr frantically tried to help them. A second shell exploded. Shrapnel ripped through Amr's stomach and exited from his back.

Amr stood up. He walked out of the tent. He collapsed. Older cousins ran towards him. They had enough gas in their car to drive Amr to Nasser Hospital, three miles away.

"Amr, are you okay?" his cousins asked.

"Yes," he moaned.

"Amr, are you awake?" they asked after a few minutes

"Yes," he whispered.

They lifted him from the car. They carried him into the overcrowded corridors of the hospital. They set him down.

THE DEATH OF AMR

He was dead.

They carried Amr's body back to the car. They drove to the family's encampment.

Amr's uncle shows me a video of Amr's mother keening over his corpse.

"My son, my son, my beloved son," she laments in the video, her left hand tenderly stroking his face. "I don't know what I will do without you."

They buried Amr in a makeshift grave.

Later that night the Israelis shelled again. Several Palestinians were wounded and killed.

The empty tent, occupied the day before by Amr's family, was obliterated.

IV.

# EXTERMINATE ALL
# THE BRUTES

Israel has destroyed hundreds of clinics, hospitals, telecommuni-cations centers, nearly all municipal and governmental buildings, commercial, industrial, and agricultural buildings, roads, homes, residential buildings, and refugee camps in Gaza.[55] The bombing of the Al-Taj tower in Gaza City on October 25, 2023, *alone* killed 101 people, including forty-four children and thirty-seven women, and injured hundreds. Israel has gutted all of Gaza's universities, along with schools and libraries. Archaeological and heritage sites, including as many as 1,000 mosques, churches, and Gaza's Cen-tral Archives, which held one hundred and fifty years of historical records and documents, are in ruins.[56]

Israel is estimated to have dropped over 83,000 tons of explo-sives—more than all the bombs dropped on Dresden, Hamburg, and London during World War II combined—on Gaza between October 7, 2023, and September 22, 2024. Many targets are selected by artificial intelligence.[57] Nearly all of Gaza's 2.3 million residents are homeless.

Hundreds of medical workers and UN workers have been killed. Doctors are forced to amputate limbs without anesthetic.[58] Those with severe medical conditions—cancer, diabetes, heart dis-ease, kidney disease—have died from lack of treatment or will die soon. In July 2024, *The Lancet*, a peer-reviewed medical journal, published an assessment of deaths caused during armed conflicts, including deaths caused by "indirect health implications beyond the direct harm from violence." The report concluded that it was "not implausible to estimate that up to 186,000 or even more" people in Palestine had been killed by Israel—including 83,000 children—from October 2023 to June 2024.[59]

Over 180 women give birth daily with little or no medical care. They are three times more likely to suffer miscarriages and—if they carry their baby to term—three times more likely to die.[60] Over ninety percent of the Palestinians in Gaza suffer from severe food insecurity with people eating animal feed and grass. Children are dying of starvation and hepatitis cases have climbed to over 40,000. In August 2024, polio was reported in Gaza.[61]

"Seventy percent of recorded deaths have consistently been women and children," writes Francesca Albanese, the United Nations Special Rapporteur on the situation of human rights in the Palestinian territories, in her report issued on March 25, 2024. "Israel failed to prove that the remaining thirty percent, i.e., adult males, were active Hamas combatants—a necessary condition for them to be lawfully targeted. By early-December, Israel's security advisors claimed the killing of '7,000 terrorists' in a stage of the campaign when less than 5,000 adult males in total had been identified among the casualties, thus implying that all adult males killed were 'terrorists.'"[62]

In a report Albanese released on October 28, 2024 she writes:

> The disturbing frequency and callousness of the killing of people known to be civilians are 'emblematic of the systematic nature' of a destructive intent.' Six-year-old Hind Rajab, killed with 355 bullets after pleading for help for hours; the fatal mauling by dogs of Muhammed Bhar, who had Down's Syndrome; the execution of Atta Ibrahim Al-Muqaid, an older deaf man, in his home, later bragged about by his killer and other soldiers on social media; the premature

babies deliberately left to die a slow death and decompose in the intensive care unit at Al-Nasr Hospital; the elderly man, Bashir Hajji, killed en route to southern Gaza after appearing in a propaganda photograph of a 'safe corridor;' Abu al-Ola, the handcuffed hostage shot by a sniper after being sent into Nasser Hospital with evacuation orders. When the dust settles on Gaza, the true extent of the horror experienced by Palestinians will become known.[63]

She chronicles how Gaza has been turned into a toxic wasteland. "Nearly 40 million tons of debris, including unexploded ordnance and human remains, contaminate the ecosystem," the report goes on. "More than 140 temporary waste sites and 340,000 tons of waste, untreated wastewater and sewage overflow contribute to the spread of diseases such as hepatitis A, respiratory infections, diarrhea and skin diseases. As Israeli leaders promised, Gaza has been made unfit for human life."[64]

Israel plays linguistic tricks to deny anyone in Gaza the status of civilians or any building—including mosques, churches, hospitals, and schools—protected status. All Palestinians are branded as responsible for the attack on October 7 or written off as human shields for Hamas. All structures are considered legitimate targets by Israel because they are allegedly Hamas command centers or said to harbor Hamas fighters.

These accusations, Albanese writes, are a "pretext" used to justify "the killing of civilians under a cloak of purported legality, whose all-enveloping pervasiveness admits only of genocidal intent."

In this decades-long conflict, we have not seen an assault by Israel on the Palestinians of this magnitude. But all these measures—the killing of civilians, dispossession of land, arbitrary detention, torture, disappearances, closures imposed on Palestinian towns and villages, house demolitions, revoking residence permits, deportation, destruction of the infrastructure that maintains civil society, military occupation, dehumanizing language, and theft of natural resources, especially aquifers—have long defined Israel's campaign to eradicate Palestinians.

The genocide in Gaza is the culmination of a process. It is not an act. The genocide is the predictable denouement of Israel's settler-colonial project. It is coded within the DNA of the Israeli apartheid state. It is where Israel had to end up. It surpasses even the worst excesses of the Nakba, or catastrophe, which saw 750,000 Palestinians driven from their land in 1948 and 8,000 to 15,000 massacred by Zionist terrorist militias such as Irgun, Lehi, Haganah, and Palmach. Israel, after its ethnic cleansing, ruled over 160,000 Palestinian Arabs who had remained, one-fifth of the pre-war Arab population.

Zionist leaders are open about their goals.

Israeli Minister of Defense Yoav Gallant, after October 7, 2023, announced that Gaza would receive "no electricity, no food, no water, no fuel."[65] Israeli Minister of Foreign Affairs Israel Katz said, "Humanitarian aid to Gaza? No electrical switch will be turned on, no water hydrant will be opened."[66] Avi Dichter, the Minister of Agriculture, referred to Israel's military assault as the "Gaza Nakba 2023."[67] Revital "Tally" Gotliv, a Likud member of the Knesset, posted on her social media account, "Bring down buildings!! Bomb without distinction!! . . . Flatten Gaza. Without mercy! This time, there is no room for mercy!"[68]

Not to be outdone, Minister of Heritage Amihai Eliyahu supported using nuclear weapons on Gaza as "one of the options."[69]

The message from the Israeli leadership is unequivocal.

Israel's playbook is the "Dahiya Doctrine." The doctrine was formulated by former Israel Defense Forces (IDF) Chief of Staff Gadi Eisenkot, who is a member of the current war cabinet, following the 2006 war between Israel and Hezbollah in Lebanon. Dahiya is a southern Beirut suburb and a Hezbollah stronghold.

It was pounded by Israeli jets after two Israeli soldiers were taken prisoner. The doctrine posits that Israel should employ massive, disproportionate force, destroying infrastructure and civilian residences, to ensure deterrence.

Daniel Hagari, spokesman of the IDF, conceded at the start of Israel's most recent attack on Gaza that the "emphasis" would be on "what causes maximum damage."[70]

Israel has abandoned its tactic of "roof knocking," where a rocket without a warhead would land on a roof to warn those inside to evacuate. Israel has also ended its phone calls warning of an impending attack. Families in an apartment block, refugee shelter, or an entire neighborhood are killed without notice.

The genocide says something not only about Israel, but about us, about Western civilization, about who we are as a people, where we came from and what defines us. It says that all our vaunted morality and respect for human rights is a lie. It says that people of color, especially when they are poor and vulnerable, do not count. It says their hopes, dreams, dignity, and aspirations for freedom are worthless. It says we will ensure global domination through racialized violence.

This lie—that Western civilization is predicated on "values" such as respect for human rights and the rule of law—is one the Palestinians, and all those in the Global South, as well as Native and Black and Brown Americans, have known for centuries.

Remember *The New York Times* columnist Thomas Friedman telling Charlie Rose on the eve of the war in Iraq that American soldiers should go house to house from Basra to Baghdad and say to Iraqis, "Suck on this?" That is the real credo of the US empire.[71]

All governments lie, as I.F. Stone pointed out, including Israel and Hamas. But Israel engages in the kinds of jaw-dropping lies that characterize despotic and totalitarian regimes. It does not deform the truth; it inverts it. It routinely paints a picture for the outside world that is diametrically opposed to reality. All of us who covered the occupied territories dutifully inserted these lies into our stories—required under the rules of American journalism—although we knew they were untrue.

I saw small boys baited and killed by Israeli soldiers in 2001 in the Gaza refugee camp of Khan Yunis. The soldiers swore at the boys in Arabic over the loudspeakers of their armored jeep. The boys, about ten years old, then threw stones at an Israeli vehicle, and the soldiers opened fire, killing some and wounding others. Such incidents, in the Israeli lexicon, become children "caught in crossfire."

I was in Gaza when attack jets struck overcrowded hovels in Gaza City. I saw the corpses of the victims, including children. This became "a surgical strike on a bomb-making factory." I have watched Israel demolish homes and entire apartment blocks to create wide buffer zones between the Palestinians and the Israeli troops that ring Gaza. Israel has now expanded its buffer zone along the Gaza perimeter to 16 percent of the territory. I have interviewed the destitute and homeless families, some camped out in crude shelters erected in the rubble. The destruction becomes the "demolition of the homes of terrorists." I have stood in the remains of schools as well as medical clinics and mosques. I have heard Israel claim that "errant rockets or mortar fire from the Palestinians" caused these and other deaths or that the locations were "being used as arms depots or launching sites."

Israel was founded on lies. The lie that Palestinian land was largely unoccupied. The lie that Palestinians fled their homes and villages during their ethnic cleansing by Zionist militias in 1948 because they were told to do so by Arab leaders. The lie that it was Arab armies that started the 1948 war that saw Israel seize seventy-eight percent of historic Palestine. The lie that Israel faced annihilation in 1967, forcing it to invade and occupy the remaining twenty-two percent of Palestine, as well as land belonging to Egypt and Syria.

Israel is sustained by lies. The lie that Israel wants a just and equitable peace and will support a Palestinian state. The lie that Israel is the "only democracy in the Middle East." The lie that Israel is an "outpost of Western civilization in a sea of barbarism." The lie that Israel respects the rule of law and human rights.

Israel's atrocities against the Palestinians are always greeted with lies. I heard them. I recorded them. I published them in my stories for *The New York Times*.

I covered war for two decades, including seven years in the Middle East. I learned quite a bit about the size and lethality of explosive devices. There is nothing in the arsenal of Hamas or Palestinian Islamic Jihad that could have replicated the massive explosive power of the missile that killed between 250 and 471 civilians in October 2023 in the Al-Ahli Baptist Hospital in Gaza, which was forcibly closed and evacuated by Israeli troops in July 2024. Nothing. If Hamas or Palestinian Islamic Jihad had these kinds of missiles, huge buildings in Israel would be rubble with hundreds of dead. They do not.

The whistling sound, audible on the video moments before the explosion on the hospital, appears to come from the high velocity of a missile. This sound gives it away. No Palestinian rocket makes this noise. And then there is the speed of the missile. Palestinian rockets are slow and lumbering, clearly visible as they arch in the sky and then tumble in free-fall toward their targets. They do not strike with precision or travel at close to supersonic speed. They are incapable of killing hundreds of people.

The Israeli military dropped "roof knocking" rockets with no warheads on the hospital in the days leading up to the strike, the familiar warning given by Israel to evacuate buildings, according to Al-Ahli Baptist Hospital officials. They also said they had received calls from Israel saying, "We warned you to evacuate twice." Israel demanded that all hospitals in northern Gaza be evacuated.

Following Israel's strike on the hospital, Hananya Naftali, a "Digital Aide" to Israeli Prime Minister Benjamin Netanyahu, posted on X: "Israeli Air Force struck a Hamas terrorist base inside a hospital in Gaza."

The post was quickly deleted.

The killing of the *Al Jazeera* journalist Shireen Abu Akleh on May 11, 2022 by the Israeli military was blamed by Israeli authorities on Palestinian gunmen. Israel disseminated footage of a Palestinian fighter they said shot and killed the journalist, who was wearing a flak jacket and helmet marked "PRESS."

Benny Gantz, who was at the time Defense Minister, stated that "no [Israeli] gunfire was directed at the journalist," and that the Israeli army had "seen footage of indiscriminate shooting by Palestinian terrorists."

This lie was peddled until video footage examined by The Israeli Center for Human Rights in the Occupied Territories (B'Tselem) identified the location of the Palestinian gunman depicted in the video. The video, the human rights organization found, was in a different location from where Shireen was killed.

When Israel is caught lying, as it was with the murder of Shireen, it promises an investigation. But these investigations are a sham. Impartial investigations into the hundreds of killings by soldiers and Jewish settlers of Palestinians are rarely carried out. Perpetrators are almost never brought to trial or held accountable. The pattern of Israeli obfuscation is predictable. So is the collusion of nearly all of the media along with Republican and Democratic politicians. US politicians decried the murder of Shireen, who was an American citizen. They dutifully repeated the old mantra, calling for a "thorough investigation" by the army that carried out the crime.

A few months later, Israel admitted that there was a "high possibility" that an Israeli soldier killed the journalist by accident.[72] By then, however, the eruption of street protests and rage over the killing of the journalist was over and her murder largely forgotten.

By the time the conclusive proof comes out about the bombing of the hospital, it too will be a distant memory.

In September 2000, *France 2 TV* captured dramatic footage of a father unsuccessfully trying to shield his traumatized twelve-year-old son, Muhammad Al-Durrah, from Israeli gunfire at the Netzarim junction in the Gaza Strip.

The killing of the boy resulted in the typical propaganda campaign by Israel. Israeli officials spent years lying about the killing, first blaming the Palestinians for the shooting, later suggesting that the scene was faked, and finally insisting the boy was still alive. When an Israeli soldier, in 2003, murdered the twenty-three-year-old American student and activist Rachel Corrie by crushing her to death with an armored military bulldozer as she tried to prevent the illegal demolition of a Palestinian doctor's home, the Israeli army said it was an accident for which Corrie was responsible.

Israel made the same claim of targeted-assassination-as-accident when an Israeli sniper shot dead the American-Turkish activist Ayşenur Ezgi Eygi on September 6, 2024. She had joined other activists to protest the theft of Palestinian farmland by Israeli colonists in the West Bank town of Beita near Nablus. The White House, refusing to ascribe blame, called on Israel to investigate. Rachel Corrie's father Craig, commenting on the murder of the twenty-six-year-old activist and yet another purported Israeli investigation, said acidly, "Israel does not do investigations; they do cover-ups."[73]

Israel blocks independent human rights organizations that investigate the atrocities and war crimes Israel commits in Gaza and the West Bank. Israel refuses to cooperate with the International Criminal Court regarding war crimes committed in the Occupied Territories. Israel does not cooperate with the UN Human Rights Council. It prohibits the UN Special Rapporteur on the occupied Palestinian territories from entering the country. In 2018, Israel revoked the work permit for Omar Shakir, the director of Human Rights Watch (Israel and Palestine), and expelled him. In May 2018, Israel's Ministry of Strategic Affairs and Public Diplomacy published a report calling on the European Union and European states to halt their direct and indirect financial support and funding to Palestinian and international human rights organizations that "have ties to terror and promote boycotts against Israel."

After the Al-Ahli Baptist bombing, Israel first released a video that purported to show Palestinian Islamic Jihad (PIJ) rockets striking the hospital. The Israelis hastily removed the video when journalists noticed that time stamps showed the images were taken forty minutes after the strike took place.

Israeli propagandists—aware that Palestinian rockets have little explosive power—then claimed that Hamas stored munitions under the hospital. This caused the massive explosion, they said. But if this were true, there would have been a secondary explosion. There was none. Israel released what they say is a recording of two Hamas militants discussing the missile strike on the hospital. The militants ask each other, in a self-incriminating conversation that is too ridiculous to believe, if Hamas or PIJ carried out the strike. *Please.* How was Israel completely in the dark about an incursion by thousands of armed Palestinian militants from Gaza into Israel on October 7, but able to capture this incriminating conversation between two supposed militants?

"Israel has a whole unit of 'mistaravim,' Israeli Jewish undercover agents trained to pose as Palestinians and secretly operate among Palestinians," the reporter Jonathan Cook writes. "Israel produced a highly popular TV series about such people in Gaza called *Fauda.* You have to be beyond credulous to think that Israel couldn't, and wouldn't, rig up a call like this to fool us, just as it regularly fools Palestinians in Gaza."[74]

Israel has also long targeted medical facilities, ambulances, and medics. It bombed a Palestinian children's hospital during the 1982 war in Lebanon, killing sixty people. It also carried out missile strikes on clearly marked Lebanese ambulances during the 2006 war between Israel and Lebanon. It damaged or destroyed twenty-nine ambulances and almost half of Gaza's health facilities, including fifteen hospitals, during the 2008–2009 assault on Gaza known as Operation Cast Lead. It routinely prohibited wounded Palestinians from being picked up by ambulances during this operation, often leaving them to die. During Operation Protective Edge, the fifty-one-day assault on Gaza in 2014, Israel destroyed or damaged seventeen hospitals, fifty-six primary healthcare centers, and forty-five ambulances.

Amnesty International, which investigated the Israeli attacks on three of these hospitals in 2014, dismissed the "evidence" for the attacks offered by Israel as false. "The image tweeted by the Israeli military does not match satellite images of the al-Wafa hospital and appears to depict a different location," the report read.[75]

Those who expose Israeli lies are banished. They are disappeared from the media and universities. They are denied forums to speak or, as has happened to me at the University of Pennsylvania, disinvited.

There is a perverted logic to Israel's repeated use of the Big Lie—*Große Lüge*—the lie favored by tyrants. The Big Lie feeds the two reactions Israel seeks to elicit: racism among its supporters and terror among its victims.

By painting a picture of an army that never attacks civilians, that indeed goes out of its way to protect them, the Big Lie says Israelis are civilized and humane, and their Palestinian opponents are inhuman monsters. The Big Lie serves the idea that the slaughter in Gaza is a clash of civilizations, a war between democracy, decency, and honor on one side and Islamic barbarism on the other. And in the cases when news of atrocities penetrates the wider public, Israel blames the destruction and casualties on Hamas.

George Orwell, in his novel *Nineteen Eighty-Four,* called this form of propaganda "doublethink." Doublethink uses "logic against logic" and "repudiate[s] morality while laying claim to it."[76] The Big Lie does not allow for the nuances and contradictions that can plague conscience. It is a state-orchestrated response to the dilemma of cognitive dissonance. The Big Lie permits no gray zones. The world is black and white, good and evil, righteous and unrighteous. The Big Lie allows believers to take comfort—a comfort they are desperately seeking—in their own moral superiority at the very moment they have abrogated all morality.

The Big Lie, as the father of American public relations, Edward Bernays, wrote, is limited only by the propagandist's capacity to fathom and harness the undercurrents of individual and mass psychology. And since most supporters of Israel do not have a desire to know the truth, a truth that would force them to examine their own racism and self-delusions about Zionist and Western moral superiority, like packs of famished dogs they lap up the lies fed to them by the Israeli government. The Big Lie always finds fertile soil in what Bernays called the "logic-proof compartment of dogmatic adherence." All effective propaganda, Bernays wrote, targets and builds upon these irrational "psychological habits."

This is the world Franz Kafka envisioned, a world where the irrational becomes rational. It is one where, as Gustave Le Bon noted in *The Crowd: A Study of the Public Mind*, those who supply the masses with the illusions they crave become their master, and "whoever attempts to destroy their illusions is always their victim."[77] This irrationality explains why the reaction of Israeli supporters to those who speak the truth is so rabid. When these voices of dissent are Jewish, it ratchets up the level of hate.

But the Big Lie is also designed to send a chilling message to Gaza's Palestinians. It makes it clear to the Palestinians that Israel will continue to wage a campaign of state terror and will never admit its atrocities or its intentions. The vast disparity between what Israel says and what Israel does tells the Palestinians that there is no hope. Israel will do and say whatever it wants. The

EXTERMINATE ALL THE BRUTES    67

truth is irrelevant. International law is irrelevant. The Palestinians are meant to understand there will never be an acknowledgement of reality by Israel.

The Big Lie destroys any possibility of history and, therefore, any hope for a dialogue between antagonistic parties that can be grounded in truth and reality. While, as Hannah Arendt pointed out, the ancient and modern sophists sought to win an argument at the expense of the truth, those who wield the Big Lie "want a more lasting victory at the expense of reality." The old sophists, she said, "destroyed the dignity of human thought." Those who resort to the Big Lie "destroy the dignity of human action."[78]

The result, Arendt warned, is that "history itself is destroyed, and its comprehensibility."[79] And when facts no longer matter, when there is no shared history grounded in the truth, when people foolishly believe their own lies, there can be no useful exchange of information. Israel's Big Lie, designed and used like a bludgeon, ultimately reduces all problems in the world to the brutish language of violence. And when oppressed people are addressed only through violence, they will answer with violence.

# V

# THE PSYCHOSIS OF PERMANENT WAR

Israel has been poisoned by the psychosis of permanent war. It sanctifies its victimhood. Human rights campaigners, intellectuals, and journalists—Israeli and Palestinian—are subject to constant state surveillance, arbitrary arrests, and government-run smear campaigns. Its educational system, starting in primary school, is an indoctrination machine for the military. The greed and corruption of its venal political and economic elite have created vast income disparities, a mirror of the decay within America's democracy, along with a culture of anti-Arab and anti-Black racism.

By the time Israel achieves its decimation of Gaza, it will have signed its own death sentence. Its facade of civility, its supposed vaunted respect for the rule of law and democracy, its mythical story of the courageous Israeli military and miraculous birth of the Jewish nation—which it successfully sold to its Western audiences—will lie in heaps of ash. Israel's social capital will be spent. It will be revealed as the ugly, repressive, hate-filled apartheid regime it always has been, alienating younger generations of American Jews. Its patron, the United States, as new generations come into power, will distance itself from Israel. Its popular support will come from reactionary Zionists and America's Christianized fascists who see Israel's domination of ancient Biblical lands as a harbinger of the Second Coming and its subjugation of Arabs as a kindred racism and celebration of white supremacy.

Settler colonialism is built on the scaffolding of racism.

Israel will become synonymous with its victims the way Turks are synonymous with the Armenians, Germans are with the Namibians and later the Jews, and Serbs are with the Bosniaks. Israel's cultural, artistic, journalistic, and intellectual life will atrophy and die. Once its mass slaughter is complete, Israel will be a despotism, a stagnant nation where religious fanatics and bigots dominate public life. It will join the club of the globe's most retrograde and despised regimes.

Despotisms can exist long after their expiration date. But they are terminal. You don't have to be a Biblical scholar to see that Israel's lust for rivers of blood is antithetical to the core values of Judaism. The cynical weaponization of the Holocaust, including branding Palestinians as Nazis, has little efficacy when you carry out a live-streamed genocide against 2.3 million people trapped in a concentration camp.

Nations need more than force to survive. They need a mystique. This mystique provides purpose, civility, and even nobility to inspire citizens to sacrifice for the nation. The mystique offers hope for the future. It provides meaning. It provides national identity.

When mystiques implode, when they are exposed as lies, a central foundation of state power collapses. I reported on the death of the communist mystiques in 1989 during the revolutions in East Germany, Czechoslovakia, and Romania. The police and the military decided there was nothing left to defend. Israel's decay will engender the same lassitude and apathy. It will not be able to recruit Indigenous collaborators, such as Mahmoud Abbas and the Palestinian Authority—detested by most Palestinians—to do their bidding.

Israel, without the United States, would probably not exist. The country came perilously close to extinction during the October 1973 war when Egypt, trained and backed by the Soviet Union, crossed the Suez, and the Syrians poured in over the Golan Heights. Huge American military transport planes came to the rescue. They began landing every half hour to refit the battered Israeli army, which had lost most of its heavy armor. By the time the war was over, the United States had given Israel $2.2 billion in emergency military aid.

The intervention, which enraged the Arab world, triggered the OPEC oil embargo that wreaked havoc on Western economies. This was perhaps the most dramatic example of the sustained life-support system the United States has provided to the Jewish state.

Israel was born at midnight on May 14, 1948. The US recognized the new state eleven minutes later.

Washington, at the beginning of the relationship, was able to be a moderating influence. An incensed President Eisenhower demanded and got Israel's withdrawal after the Israelis occupied Gaza in 1956. During the Six-Day War in 1967, Israeli warplanes bombed the USS Liberty. The ship, flying the US flag and stationed fifteen miles off the Israeli coast, was intercepting tactical and strategic communications from both sides. It would have likely known that Israel had executed captured Egyptian soldiers and buried them in mass graves. The Israeli strikes killed thirty-four US sailors and wounded 171. The deliberate attack froze, for a while, Washington's enthusiasm for Israel. But ruptures like this one proved to be only bumps, soon smoothed out by an increasingly sophisticated and well-financed Israel lobby that set out to merge Israeli and American foreign policy in the Middle East.

Israel has reaped tremendous rewards from this alliance. It has been given more than $140 billion in US direct economic and military assistance. It receives over $3 billion in direct assistance annually, roughly one-fifth of the US foreign aid budget.[80] Although most American foreign aid packages stipulate that related military purchases have to be made in the United States,

Israel is allowed to use about twenty-five percent of the money to subsidize its own growing and profitable armaments industry. It is exempt, unlike other nations, from accounting for how it spends the aid money. And funds are routinely siphoned off to build new Jewish settlements and bolster the Israeli occupation in the Palestinian territories.

The US, as John Mearsheimer and Stephen Walt point out, has provided Israel with nearly $3 billion to develop weapons systems. It has given Israel access to some of the most sophisticated items in its military arsenal, including Blackhawk attack helicopters and F-35 fighter jets. The United States, they add, "also gives Israel access to intelligence it denies to its NATO allies." And when Israel refused to sign The Treaty on the Non-Proliferation of Nuclear Weapons, the US government stood by without a word of protest as the Israelis built the region's first nuclear weapons program.[81]

United States foreign policy in the Middle East has become little more than an extension of Israeli foreign policy. The US has vetoed a total of eighty-six United Nations Security Council resolutions since it cast its first-ever veto in 1970. Over half—forty-five of all the UN Security Council resolutions the US has vetoed— were critical of Israel.[82] At the same time, it refuses to enforce the Security Council resolutions it claims to support, calling for an end to Israel's occupation.

Few in the Middle East see any distinction between Israeli and American policies, nor should they. When the Islamic radicals speak of US support of Israel as a prime reason for their hatred of the United States, we should listen. The consequences of this one-sided relationship were played out in the disastrous war in Iraq, which Israel advocated. This special relationship is at the center of escalating tensions with Lebanon, Syria, Yemen, Iraq, and Iran, and the genocide in Gaza.

US foreign policy in the Middle East is unraveling because of this special relationship.

Some in the US establishment and State Department saw this situation coming. The decision to throw our lot in with Israel was not initially a popular one with an array of foreign policy experts, including Harry Truman's Secretary of State, General George Marshall. They warned there would be a backlash. They knew the price the United States would pay for this decision in the oil-rich region, which they feared would be one of the greatest strategic blunders of the postwar era. And they were right.

The alliance, which makes no sense in geopolitical terms, does make sense when seen through the lens of domestic politics. Israel's lobby is a potent force in the American political system. No major candidate, Democrat or Republican, dares to challenge it. The Israeli lobby successfully purged the State Department of Arab experts who challenged the notion that Israeli and American interests were identical. Backers of Israel have doled out hundreds of millions of dollars to support US political candidates deemed favorable to Israel. They have brutally punished those who strayed, including the first president Bush, who they said was not vigorous enough in his defense of Israeli interests. This was a lesson the second Bush White House did not forget. George W. Bush did not want to be a one-term president like his father.

Israel advocated removing Saddam Hussein from power, which turned out to be a quagmire for the US military, and continues to advocate for war with Iran, ostensibly to prevent it from acquiring nuclear weapons, but also to degrade it as a regional power. During the Cold War, the United States avoided direct military involvement in the region. Now it does the bidding of Israel, plunging into one military fiasco after another.

The United States, at least officially, does not support Israel's occupation and calls for a viable Palestinian state. It is a global player with interests that stretch well beyond the boundaries of the Middle East, and the equation that Israel's enemies are our enemies is not that simple.

"Terrorism is not a single adversary," Mearsheimer and Walt write in *The London Review of Books*, "but a tactic employed by a wide array of political groups. The terrorist organizations that threaten Israel do not threaten the United States, except when it intervenes against them (as in Lebanon in 1982). Moreover, Palestinian terrorism is not random violence directed against Israel or 'the West'; it is largely a response to Israel's prolonged campaign to colonize the West Bank and Gaza Strip. More important, saying that Israel and the US are united by a shared terrorist threat has the causal relationship backwards: the US has a terrorism problem in good part because it is so closely allied with Israel, not the other way around."[83]

Tolerance for Israeli crimes, however, is running out.

The International Court of Justice (ICJ) refused to implement the most crucial demand made by South African jurists: "The State of Israel shall immediately suspend its military operations in and against Gaza."[84] But at the same time, it delivered a devastating blow to the foundational myth of Israel. Israel, which paints itself as eternally persecuted, was credibly accused of committing genocide against Palestinians in Gaza in 2024.

Palestinians are the victims, not the perpetrators, of the "crime of crimes." A people, once in need of protection from genocide, are now committing it. The court's January 2024 ruling questions the very raison d'être of the "Jewish State" and challenges the impunity Israel has enjoyed since its founding in 1948.

The ICJ ordered Israel to take six provisional measures to prevent acts of genocide, measures that would be very difficult, if not impossible, to fulfill as Israel continues its saturation bombing of Gaza and wholesale targeting of vital infrastructure.

The court called on Israel "to prevent and punish the direct and public incitement to commit genocide." It demanded Israel "take immediate and effective measures to enable the provision of urgently needed basic services and humanitarian assistance." It ordered Israel to protect Palestinian civilians. It called on Israel to protect the 50,000 pregnant women in Gaza. It ordered Israel to take "effective measures to prevent the destruction and ensure the preservation of evidence related to allegations of acts within the scope of Article II and Article III of the Convention on the Prevention and Punishment of the Crime of Genocide against members of the Palestinian group in the Gaza Strip."[85]

The court ordered Israel to "take all measures within its power" to prevent the crimes which amount to genocide, such as "killing, causing serious bodily and mental harm, inflicting on the group conditions of life calculated to bring about its physical destruction in whole or in part, and imposing measures intended to prevent births within the group."[86]

Israel was ordered to report back to explain what it had done to implement the provisional measures.

Gaza was pounded with bombs, missiles, and artillery shells as the ruling was read in The Hague.

Translated into the vernacular, the court said Israel must feed and provide medical care for the victims, cease public statements advocating genocide, preserve evidence of genocide and stop killing Palestinian civilians.

It was hard to see how these provisional measures could be achieved as the carnage in Gaza continued.

"Without a ceasefire, the order doesn't actually work," Naledi Pandor, South Africa's Minister of International Relations, stated bluntly after the ruling.[87]

At best, the court—while it will not rule for a few years on whether Israel is committing genocide—has given legal license to use the word "genocide" to describe what Israel is doing in Gaza.

The only significant resistance to the genocide has been provided by Yemen's Red Sea blockade. Yemen, which was under siege for eight years by Saudi Arabia, the United Arab Emirates, France, the United Kingdom, and the United States, suffered over

400,000 deaths from starvation, lack of health care, infectious diseases, and the deliberate bombing of schools, hospitals, infrastructure, residential areas, markets, funerals, and weddings. Since at least 2017, multiple UN agencies have described Yemen as experiencing "the largest humanitarian crisis in the world." They know all too well what the Palestinians are enduring.

When the history of this genocide is written, Yemen's resistance will set it apart from nearly every other nation. Most of the Arab world retreats into toothless rhetorical condemnations or actively supports Israel's obliteration of Gaza and its 2.3 million inhabitants by opening up land routes through Jordan, Saudi Arabia, and the United Arab Emirates to compensate for the maritime blockade.

The Jewish Institute for National Security Affairs, a pro-Israel think tank based in Washington D.C., reported on July 23, 2024, that from October 2023 to July 2024, the US sent Israel thousands of metric tons of weapons and supplies including: 52,229 artillery rounds, 44,000 automatic rifles, 13,981 high-explosive anti-tank rounds, 14,000 tank rounds, 200 switchblade armed "kamikaze" drones, vehicles, 22,400 unguided bombs ranging from 500 to 2,000 pounds, $500 million worth of tactical vehicles and around seventy-five fighter jets.[88]

US weapons and military equipment are being shipped to Israel—which is running out of munitions—from the British base RAF Akrotiri in Cyprus, according to the U.K. investigative website *Declassified UK.* The Israeli newspaper *Haaretz* reported that more than forty US and twenty British transport aircraft, along with seven heavy-lift helicopters, have flown into RAF Akrotiri, a forty-minute flight from Tel Aviv.

Germany, which provides around thirty percent of Israel's military imports, fast-tracked armaments exports following October 7, including 500,000 rounds of ammunition for automatic or semi-automatic guns and 3,000 portable anti-tank weapons.[89]

In April, the US government's own experts published two separate confidential reports concluding that the state of Israel was deliberately preventing food and medicine from entering Gaza, and that weapons shipments should be suspended, the investigative news organization ProPublica revealed in September.[90]

The United States Agency for International Development provided Secretary of State Antony Blinken a "detailed seventeen-page memo on Israel's conduct" which described "instances of Israeli interference with aid efforts, including killing aid workers, razing agricultural structures, bombing ambulances and hospitals, sitting on supply depots and routinely turning away trucks full of food and medicine," the news outlet reported.[91]

"Separately, the head of the State Department's Bureau of Population, Refugees and Migration had also determined that Israel was blocking humanitarian aid and that the Foreign Assistance Act should be triggered to freeze almost $830 million in taxpayer dollars earmarked for weapons and bombs to Israel, according to emails obtained by ProPublica."[92]

Yet both the President and the Secretary of State refused to accept their findings and failed to disclose them to the public.

Instead, the following month, Secretary Blinken told Congress, "We do not currently assess that the Israeli government is prohibiting or otherwise restricting the transport or delivery of US humanitarian assistance."[93]

If the ICJ rules against Israel in its final judgment, countries such as the US, the UK, and Germany will be recognized by the world's most important international court as accomplices to genocide.

The ICJ's interim order and conclusion that it was "plausible" that Israel was engaged in genocide was dismissed by Israeli leaders.

Prime Minister Benjamin Netanyahu, seeking to paint the decision not to demand a ceasefire as a victory for Israel, said, "Like every country, Israel has an inherent right to defend itself.

The vile attempt to deny Israel this fundamental right is blatant discrimination against the Jewish state, and it was justly rejected. The charge of genocide leveled against Israel is not only false, it's outrageous, and decent people everywhere should reject it."[94]

"The decision of the antisemitic court in The Hague proves what was already known: This court does not seek justice, but rather the persecution of Jewish people," National Security Minister Itamar Ben-Gvir said. "They were silent during the Holocaust and today they continue the hypocrisy and take it another step further."[95]

The ICJ was founded in 1945 following the Nazi Holocaust. The first case it heard was submitted to the court in 1947.

"Decisions that endanger the continued existence of the State of Israel must not be listened to," Ben-Gvir added. "We must continue defeating the enemy until complete victory."[96]

The court, which rejected Israel's arguments to dismiss the case, acknowledged "that the military operation being conducted by Israel following the attack of 7 October 2023 has resulted, *inter alia*, in tens of thousands of deaths and injuries and the destruction of homes, schools, medical facilities, and other vital infrastructure, as well as displacement on a massive scale."

The ruling included a statement made by the UN Under-Secretary-General for Humanitarian Affairs and Emergency Relief Coordinator, Martin Griffiths, who, on January 5, 2024, called Gaza "a place of death and despair." The court document went on:

> . . . Families are sleeping in the open as temperatures plummet. Areas where civilians were told to relocate for their safety have come under bombardment. Medical facilities are under relentless attack. The few hospitals that are partially functional are overwhelmed with trauma cases, critically short of all supplies, and inundated by desperate people seeking safety.

A public health disaster is unfolding. Infectious diseases are spreading in overcrowded shelters as sewers spill over. Some 180 Palestinian women are giving birth daily amidst this chaos. People are facing the highest levels of food insecurity ever recorded. Famine is around the corner.

For children in particular, the past twelve weeks have been traumatic: No food. No water. No school. Nothing but the terrifying sounds of war, day in and day out.

Gaza has simply become uninhabitable. Its people are witnessing daily threats to their very existence—while the world watches on.[97]

The court acknowledged that "an unprecedented ninety-three percent of the population in Gaza is facing crisis levels of hunger, with insufficient food and high levels of malnutrition. At least one in four households are facing 'catastrophic conditions': experiencing an extreme lack of food and starvation and having resorted to selling off their possessions and other extreme measures to afford a simple meal. Starvation, destitution, and death are evident."[98]

The court order, quoting Philippe Lazzarini, the Commissioner-General of the United Nations Relief and Works Agency for Palestine Refugees in the Near East (UNRWA), continued:

Overcrowded and unsanitary UNRWA shelters have now become "home" to more than 1.4 million people. They lack everything, from food to hygiene to privacy. People live in inhumane conditions, where diseases are spreading, including among children. They live through the unlivable, with the clock ticking fast towards famine.

The plight of children in Gaza is especially heartbreaking. An entire generation of children is traumatized and will take years to heal. Thousands have been killed, maimed, and orphaned. Hundreds of thousands are deprived of education. Their future is in jeopardy, with far-reaching and long-lasting consequences.[99]

On October 28, 2024, the Israeli parliament approved a bill to ban UNRWA, a lifeline for Palestinians in Gaza, from operating on Israeli territory and areas under Israel's control. The ban almost certainly ensures the collapse of aid distribution, already crippled, in Gaza.

The court also referred pointedly to comments made by multiple senior Israeli government officials advocating genocide, including the President and Minister of Defense. Statements made by government and other officials form a crucial element of the "intent" component when seeking to establish the crime of genocide.

It quoted Israeli Defense Minister Yoav Gallant who declared—two days after the Hamas-led attack of October 7—that he ordered a "complete siege" of Gaza City with "no electricity, no food, no fuel" being permitted.

"I have released all restraints . . . You saw what we are fighting against. We are fighting human animals. This is the ISIS of Gaza," Gallant told Israeli troops massing around Gaza the following day. "This is what we are fighting against . . . Gaza won't return to what it was before. There will be no Hamas. We will eliminate everything. If it doesn't take one day, it will take a week, it will take weeks or even months, we will reach all places."[100]

The ICJ quoted Israel's President Isaac Herzog as saying, "It is not true this rhetoric about civilians not aware, not involved. It is absolutely not true. They could have risen up. They could have fought against that evil regime which took over Gaza in a coup d'état. But we are at war. We are at war. We are defending our homes." Herzog continued, "We are protecting our homes. That's the truth. And when a nation protects its home, it fights. And we will fight until we'll break their backbone."[101]

"A deep and wide moral abyss separates us from our enemies," Netanyahu said of the Palestinians. "They sanctify death while we sanctify life. They sanctify cruelty while we sanctify compassion."[102]

The decision was read out by the ICJ's current president, Judge Joan Donoghue, an American lawyer who used to work at the US State Department and the Department of the Treasury before she joined the World Court in 2010.

"In the Court's view, the facts and circumstances mentioned above are sufficient to conclude that at least some of the rights claimed by South Africa and for which it is seeking protection are plausible," it read. "This is the case with respect to the right of the Palestinians in Gaza to be protected from acts of genocide and related prohibited acts identified in Article III, and the right of South Africa to seek Israel's compliance with the latter's obligations under the Convention."[103]

It is clear from the ruling that the court is fully aware of the magnitude of Israel's crimes. This makes the decision not to call for the immediate suspension of Israeli military activity in and against Gaza all the more distressing.

The future is ominous. Not only do Israel's foreign policy objectives not coincide with American interests, they actively hurt them. The growing belligerence in the Middle East, the calls for an attack against Iran, which does not threaten the US, the collapse of the imperial project in Iraq have all given an opening, where there was none before, to America's rivals. It is not in Israel's interests to ignite a regional conflict. It is not in ours. But those who have their hands on the wheel seem determined to keep the American ship of state headed at breakneck speed into the cliffs.

The Latin word *extermino* translates into "drive over the border." It is combined with the word *terminus*, which means "exile, banish, exclude," to form the English word exterminate— literally to "drive over the border to death, banish from life."[104]

A new world is being born. It is a world where the old rules, more often honored in the breach than the observance, no longer matter. It is a world where wealthy nations with vast bureaucratic structures and technologically advanced military systems carry out campaigns of extermination. The industrialized nations, weakened, fearful of global chaos, by backing Israel, are sending an ominous message to the Global South and anyone who might think of revolt: we will kill you without restraint.

As climate change imperils survival, as resources become scarce, as migration becomes an imperative for millions, as agricultural yields decline, as coastal areas are flooded, as droughts and wild fires proliferate, as states fail, as armed resistance movements rise to battle their oppressors along with their proxies, genocide will not be an anomaly. It will be the norm. The industrial nations do not yet employ the dehumanizing rhetoric adopted by Israeli leaders to describe the desperate billions in the Global South. But that day is coming, and with it, the genocidal slaughter of those Frantz Fanon calls "the wretched of the earth."

One day, we will all be Palestinians.

# VI

# THE ERASURE OF THE PALESTINIANS

I have covered urban warfare in El Salvador, Iraq, Gaza, Bosnia, and Kosovo. Once you fight street by street, apartment block by apartment block, there is only one rule: kill anything that moves. The talk of safe zones, the reassurances of protecting civilians, the promises of "surgical" and "targeted" air strikes, the establishment of "safe" evacuation routes, the fatuous explanation that civilian dead were "caught in the crossfire," the claim that the homes and apartment buildings bombed into rubble were the abode of terrorists or that errant Hamas rockets were responsible for the destruction of schools and hospitals, are all part of the rhetorical cover to carry out indiscriminate slaughter.

During the siege in Sarajevo, when I was reporting for *The New York Times*, we never endured the level of saturation bombing and near total blockage of food, water, fuel, and medicine that Israel has imposed on Gaza. We never endured hundreds of dead and wounded a day. We never endured the complicity of the international community in the Serbian campaign of genocide. We never endured Washington intervening to block ceasefire resolutions. We never endured massive arms shipments from the US and other Western countries to sustain the siege. We never endured press reports from Sarajevo that were routinely discredited and dismissed by the international community, although twenty-five journalists were killed in the war by the besieging Serbian forces.

We never endured Western governments justifying the siege as the right of the Serbs to defend themselves, although the UN peacekeepers sent to Bosnia were largely a public relations gesture, ineffective in halting the slaughter until forced to respond following the massacre of 8,000 Bosniak men and boys at Srebrenica.

I don't mean to minimize the horror of the siege of Sarajevo, which gives me nightmares nearly three decades later. But what we suffered—three to four hundred shells a day, four to five dead a day, and two dozen wounded a day—is a tiny fraction of the wholesale death and destruction in Gaza. The Israeli siege of Gaza more resembles the Wehrmacht's assault on Stalingrad, where over ninety percent of the city's buildings were destroyed, than Sarajevo.

Israel seeks to erase not only the Palestinians as a people, but the idea of Palestine. And like other perpetrators of genocide, Israel intends to keep it hidden.

"This is a unique colonialism that we've been subjected to where they have no use for us," Edward Said commented. "The best Palestinian for them is either dead or gone. It's not that they want to exploit us, or that they need to keep us there in the way of Algeria or South Africa as a subclass."[105]

Israel's distorted settler-colonial visage mirrors our own in the West. We ascribe to ourselves virtues and civilizing qualities that are, as in Israel, flimsy justifications for stripping an occupied and besieged people of their rights, seizing their land, and using prolonged imprisonment, torture, humiliation, enforced poverty, and murder to keep them subjugated.

Our past, including our recent past in the Middle East, is built on the idea of subduing or wiping out the "inferior" races of the earth. We give these "inferior" races names that embody evil. ISIS. Al-Qaeda. Hezbollah. The Houthis. Hamas. We use racist slurs to dehumanize them. "Haji." "Sand N*gger." "Camel Jockey."

"Ali Baba." "Dung Shoveler." And then, because they embody evil, because they are less than human, we feel licensed, as Nissim Vaturi, a member of the Israeli parliament for the Likud party said, to erase "the Gaza Strip from the face of the earth."[106]

Naftali Bennett, Israel's former Prime Minister, in an interview on *Sky News* said, "We're fighting Nazis." In other words, absolute evil.[107]

Not to be outdone, Prime Minister Benjamin Netanyahu described Hamas in a press conference with the German Chancellor Olaf Scholz, as "the new Nazis."[108]

Think about that. A people, imprisoned in the world's largest concentration camp for seventeen years—denied food, water, fuel, and medicine, lacking an army, air force, navy, mechanized units, artillery, command and control, or missile batteries—is being butchered and starved by one of the most advanced militaries on the planet, and *they* are the Nazis?

There is a historical analogy here. But it is not one that Bennett, Netanyahu, or any other Israeli leader wants to acknowledge.

When those who are occupied refuse to submit, when they continue to resist, we drop all pretense of our "civilizing" mission and unleash, as in Gaza, an orgy of slaughter and destruction. We become drunk on violence. This violence makes us insane. We kill with reckless ferocity. We become the beasts we accuse the oppressed of being. We expose the lie of our vaunted moral superiority. We expose the fundamental truth about Western civilization: we are the most ruthless and efficient killers on the planet. This alone ensures our domination. It has nothing to do with democracy or freedom or liberty. These are rights we never intend to grant to the oppressed.

"Honor, justice, compassion, and freedom are ideas that have no converts," Joseph Conrad writes. "There are only people, without knowing, understanding, or feelings, who intoxicate themselves with words, repeat words, shout them out, imagining they believe them without believing in anything else but profit, personal advantage, and their own satisfaction."[109]

Genocide is the core of Western colonialism. It is not unique to Israel. It is not unique to the Nazis. It is the building block of Western domination. The "humanitarian interventionists" who insist we should bomb and occupy other nations because we embody goodness—although they promote military intervention only when it is perceived to be in our national interest—are useful idiots of the war machine and global imperialists. They live in an Alice-in-Wonderland fairytale where the rivers of blood we spawn make the world a happier and better place. They are the smiley faces of genocide. You can watch them on your screens. You can listen to them spout their pseudo-morality in the White House and in Congress. You can read their books. They are always wrong. And they never go away.

Maybe we are fooled by our own lies, but most of the world sees us, and Israel, clearly. They understand our rank hypocrisy and self-righteousness. They see that Palestinians, without power, forced to live in squalid refugee camps or the diaspora, denied their homeland and persecuted, suffer the kind of fate once reserved for Jews. This, perhaps, is the final tragic irony. A people that was once in need of protection from genocide now commits it.

All Israel has left is escalating savagery, including torture and lethal violence against unarmed civilians, which accelerates the decline. This wholesale violence works in the short term, as it did in the war waged by the French in Algeria, the Dirty War waged by Argentina's military dictatorship, the British occupation of India, Egypt, Kenya, and Northern Ireland, and the American occupations of Vietnam, Iraq, and Afghanistan. But in the long term, it is suicidal. The genocide in Gaza has produced a new generation of deeply traumatized and enraged young men and women whose families have been killed and whose communities have been obliterated. They are prepared to take the place of martyred leaders.

This attack is the final Israeli push to extinguish a Palestinian state and crush or expel the Palestinian people. The images of dead Palestinian children, lined up as if asleep, are a metaphor for the future. Israel speaks to the Palestinians in the language of death. And the language of death is all the Palestinians will be able to speak back. The slaughter—let's stop pretending this is a war—is empowering an array of radical Islamists. It is demolishing the shaky foundations of the corrupt secular Arab regimes on Israel's borders, including in Egypt and Jordan.

Hamas cannot lose this conflict. Militant movements feed off martyrs, and Israel is delivering the maimed and the dead by the truckload. Hamas fighters, armed with little more than light weapons, a few rockets, and small mortars, are battling one of the most sophisticated military machines on the planet. And the determined resistance by these doomed fighters exposes, throughout the Arab world, the gutlessness of dictators like Egypt's Abdel Fattah Al-Sisi, who refuses to open Egypt's border with Gaza, and Jordan's King Abdullah, who permits trucks to ship products into Israel to compensate for the disruption in maritime traffic by Yemen.

Israel, when it bombed Lebanon in 2006, sought to destroy Hezbollah. By the time it withdrew it had swelled Hezbollah's power base and handed it heroic status throughout the Arab world. Israel is now doing the same for Hamas.

The refusal by political leaders and nearly every member of the US Congress to speak out in defense of the rule of law and fundamental human rights exposes our cowardice and hypocrisy.

Uri Avnery was born in Germany. He moved to Palestine as a young boy with his parents. He left school at the age of fourteen and a year later joined the underground Jewish paramilitary group known as the Irgun. Four years later, disgusted with its use of violence, he walked away from the clandestine organization, which carried out terrorist attacks on British occupation authorities and Palestinians.

"You can't tell me about terrorism, I was a terrorist," he says when confronted with his persistent calls for peace with the Palestinians.

Avnery was a fighter in the Samson's Foxes commando unit during the 1948 war. He wrote the elite unit's anthem. After the war he became a force for left-wing politics in Israel and one of the country's most prominent journalists, running the alternative *HaOlam HaZeh* magazine. He served in the Israeli Knesset. During the 1982 siege of Beirut, in open defiance of Israeli law, he met with Palestine Liberation Organization (PLO) leader Yasser Arafat. He routinely joined Arab protesters in Israel and condemned what he called Israel's "instinct of using force" with the Palestinians and the "moral insanity" of the attacks on Gaza.

Avnery, who died at the age of ninety-four in 2018, was seriously wounded in an assassination attempt in 1975 by an Israeli. In 2006, the right-wing activist Baruch Marzel called on the Israeli military to carry out a targeted assassination of him.

"The state of Israel, like any other state," Avnery told me, "cannot tolerate having its citizens shelled, bombed, or rocketed, but there has been no thought as to how to solve the problem through political means or to analyze where this phenomenon has come from, what has caused it. Israelis, as a whole, cannot put themselves in the shoes of others. We are too self-centered. We cannot stand in the shoes of Palestinians or Arabs to ask how we would react in the same situation. Sometimes, very rarely, it happens. Years ago when Ehud Barak was asked how he would behave if he were a Palestinian, he said, 'I would join a terrorist organization.' If you do not understand Hamas, if you do not understand why Hamas does what it does, if you don't understand Palestinians, you take recourse in brute force."

The public debate about the Gaza slaughter engages in the absurd pretense that it is Israel, not the Palestinians, whose security and dignity are being threatened. This blind defense of Israeli brutality toward the Palestinians betrays the memory of those killed in other genocides, from the Holocaust to Cambodia to Rwanda to Bosnia.

Palestinians are being slaughtered with American-made weapons. But perhaps our callous indifference to human suffering is to be expected. We, after all, killed women and children on an even vaster scale in Iraq and Afghanistan. The bloody hands of Israel mirror our own.

There will be more dead Palestinian children. There will be more UN schools used as sanctuaries for terrified families, blown to bits by Israeli shells, killing women and children. There will be more emaciated, orphaned children. There will be more screaming or comatose patients on the floors of Gaza's glutted hospital corridors. And there will be more absurd news reports that parrot Israeli lies.

The cynicism of conveying propaganda as truth, as long as it is well-sourced, is the poison of American journalism. If this is all journalism has become, if moral outrage, the courage to defy the powerful, and the commitment to tell the truth and give a voice to those who without us would have no voice no longer matter, our journalism schools should focus exclusively on shorthand. It seems to be the skill most ardently coveted by those who own the commercial media.

There have always been Israeli leaders, since the inception of the state, who have called for the total physical removal of the Palestinians. The ethnic cleansing of Palestinians in 1948 and 1967 was, for them, only the beginning.

"It seems," Ilan Pappé writes, "that even the most horrendous crimes, such as the genocide in Gaza, are treated as discrete events, unconnected to anything that happened in the past and not associated with any ideology or system. Very much as the apartheid ideology explained the oppressive policies of the South African government, this ideology—in its most consensual and simplistic variety—has allowed all the Israeli governments in the past and the present to dehumanize the Palestinians wherever they are and strive to destroy them. The means altered from period to period, from location to location, as did the narrative covering up these atrocities. But there is a clear pattern [of genocide]."[110]

Israel's destruction of Gaza will not bring peace or security to Israel. If it continues, it will merely obliterate the only internal organization with enough stature and authority in Gaza to maintain order, opening a Pandora's box of ills.

# VII

# THE SLAVE REVOLT

Collective retribution against innocents is a familiar tactic employed by colonial rulers. We used it against Native Americans and later in the Philippines and Vietnam. The Germans used it against the Herero and Namaqua in Namibia. The British in Kenya and Malaya. The Nazis used it in the areas they occupied in the Soviet Union and Eastern and Central Europe. Israel follows the same playbook. Death for death. Atrocity for atrocity. But it is always the occupier who initiates this macabre dance and trades piles of corpses for higher piles of corpses.

This is not to defend the war crimes by either side. It is not to rejoice in the attacks. I have seen enough violence to loathe it. But this is the familiar denouement to all settler-colonial projects.

Regimes implanted and maintained by violence engender violence. The Haitian war of liberation. The Mau Mau in Kenya. The African National Congress in South Africa. These uprisings do not always succeed, but they follow familiar patterns. The Palestinians, like all occupied people, have a right to armed resistance under international law.

How can you trap 2.3 million people in Gaza, half of whom are unemployed, in one of the most densely populated places on the planet; reduce the lives of its residents, half of whom are children, to a subsistence level; deprive them of basic medical supplies, food, water, and electricity; use attack aircraft, artillery, mechanized units, missiles, naval guns, and infantry units to randomly slaughter unarmed civilians; and not expect a violent response?

Many of the resistance fighters who infiltrated Israel on October 7, 2023 undoubtedly knew they would be killed. However, like resistance fighters in other wars of liberation, they decided that if they could not choose how they would live, they would choose how they would die.

Norman Finkelstein, one of the foremost scholars on Israel-Palestine, draws parallels between the October 7 attack and the 1831 Nat Turner Rebellion, which was the largest slave rebellion in the United States.

"Nat Turner was a religious fanatic," Finkelstein told me. "Incidentally, so was John Brown. We'll stick now to Nat Turner. Each of them was convinced that they were acting on God's word, that they were agents of God and they were doing God's will. Their actions were sanctioned by God. You might call them premature jihadis. That's what they were. And it's reported in *Nat Turner's Fierce Rebellion* by Stephen Oates—a very respected historian—that Nat Turner gave the order to his federates to kill all whites. Part of it was revenge, for sure, but he wanted to create a moral crisis to force the country to confront the reality of slavery."

Nat Turner's four-day slave revolt killed fifty-five white civilians, including men, women, and children.

"John Brown hacked to death civilians," Finkelstein went on. "Frederick Douglass gave this absolutely breathtaking speech on John Brown. He had come to grips with the question of killing civilians. Du Bois wrote a biography of John Brown, not very good, but there weren't many resources to draw from. He, too, in the last chapter, confronts the question of John Brown and the killing of civilians. Neither of them condemned Brown. They circled around it. They recognized they had to confront this question, but they wouldn't condemn John Brown for killing civilians.

"My regard for the abolitionists went through the roof when

THE SLAVE REVOLT 93

I read what William Lloyd Garrison wrote," he continued. "He acknowledged the horror that had occurred. But he very studiously and carefully would not condemn the Nat Turner rebellion. He condemned all the hypocrites who were condemning the rebellion. And he said we told you so. We told you so. We warned you. We warned you. We warned you that you were going to drive these people mad and they're going to do something horrible. I read it, and I reread it and I reread it.

"In the past couple of days, I had to refresh my memory of my own book," Finkelstein said. "I started to reread my book, *Gaza: An Inquest into its Martyrdom*. I'm telling you, honest to God, I began to get so filled with rage as I went through each detail of what was done to those people. Two things: Number one, I understand now why Garrison did not condemn the rebellion. Because he saw [slavery] day in and day out. Unlike Gaza, slavery was not out of sight. He saw day in and day out the humiliation, the degradation, the physical assault on the people, the African-American slaves, and he realized he could not in good conscience condemn them for what they did.

"I can understand being driven mad," Finkelstein went on. "Driven mad by being born into a concentration camp, never seeing anything except what is within twenty-five miles by five miles. No hope at all. Everybody had abandoned them on October 7. The US administration and Israel were cobbling together an agreement with Saudi Arabia to end the Arab-Israeli conflict and leave the Palestinians, in particular in Gaza, to languish and die. That's where we stood."

The Palestinians are treated as human laboratory rats by the Israeli military, intelligence services, and arms and technology industries. Israel's drones, and surveillance technology—including spyware, facial recognition software, and biometric gathering infrastructure—along with smart fences, experimental bombs, and AI-controlled machine guns, are tested on the captive population in Gaza, often with lethal results. These weapons and technologies are then certified as "battle-tested" and sold around the world.

Israel is the tenth biggest arms dealer on the planet and sells its technology and weapons to an estimated one hundred and thirty nations, including military dictatorships in Asia and Latin America. Israeli weapons sales totaled $13 billion in 2023.[111] Its close relationship with these military, internal security, surveillance, intelligence-gathering, and law enforcement agencies explains the fulsome support Israel's allies give to its genocidal campaign in Gaza.

When Colombian President Gustavo Petro refused to condemn the October 7 attack as a "terrorist attack" and said, "terrorism is killing innocent children in Palestine," Israel immediately halted all sales of military and security equipment to Colombia. This global cabal, dedicated to permanent war and keeping its populations monitored and controlled, makes hundreds of billions of dollars a year in sales. These technologies are cementing into place a supranational corporate totalitarianism, a world where populations are enslaved in ways that past totalitarian regimes could only imagine.

Israel, which is not a signatory of the Arms Trade Treaty, has long supplied some of the most heinous regimes on the planet with weaponry, including the apartheid governments of South Africa and Myanmar. India is Israel's largest purchaser of military drones. Israel provided Unmanned Aerial Vehicles (UAVs), missiles, and mortars to Azerbaijan for its invasion and occupation of Nagorno-Karabakh, which displaced 100,000 people, more than eighty percent of the enclave's ethnic Armenians. Israel sold napalm and weapons to the Salvadoran military, as well as the murderous regime of General José Efraín Ríos Montt in Guatemala, when I covered the wars in the 1980s in Central America.[112] Israeli-made Uzi submachine guns were the weapons of choice for Central American death squads. Israel also sold weapons to the Bosnian Serbs, despite international sanctions, when I covered the war in Bosnia in the 1990s, a conflict that took the lives of 100,000 people.[113]

"Israel is a key player in the EU [European Union] battle to both militarize its borders and deter new arrivals, a policy that hugely accelerated after the massive influx of migrants in 2015, principally due to the wars in Syria, Iraq, and Afghanistan," writes Antony Loewenstein in *The Palestine Laboratory: How Israel Exports the Technology of Occupation Around the World.* "The EU has partnered with leading Israeli defense companies to use its drones, and of course years of experience in Palestine is a key selling point," he explains.[114]

"The similarities between the US-Mexico border and Israel's wall through the occupied territories are growing by the year," Loewenstein continues. "One informs and inspires the other, with tech companies always looking for new ways to target and capture perceived enemies. The use of high-tech surveillance tools to monitor the border was backed by both Republicans and Democrats. One company during the Trump years, Brinc (backed by the billionaire Peter Thiel), tested the possibility of deploying armed drones that would taser migrants with a stun gun along the US–Mexico border."[115]

The Hermes 900 and the Heron TP "Eitan" drones, manufactured by Elbit Systems and Israel Aerospace Industries respectively—Israel's two largest weapons manufacturers and exporters—are used by Frontex, the European Union's external border and coastal agency, to monitor and deter migrant and refugee boats in the Mediterranean. Both drones can be armed, and the Heron TP, which can fly for up to forty hours continuously, can be modified to carry four Spike rockets with fragmentation sleeves of thousands of 3mm tungsten cubes that puncture metal and "cause tissue to be torn from flesh"—in essence, shredding the victim. They are routinely used on Palestinians.

"It's almost impossible to cross the Mediterranean [as a migrant]," Felix Weiss, of the German NGO Sea-Watch, told Loewenstein. "Frontex has become a militarized actor, its equipment coming from war zones," he added.[116]

Elbit Systems, Israel's largest private weapons firm, supplies US Customs and Border Protection (CBP) with high-tech surveillance towers which it uses along the border with Mexico. It also supplied the CBP with its Hermes drone in 2004 to test the feasibility of using UAVs on the border.

Pegasus, a phone-hacking tool produced by the Israeli technology firm NSO Group was used by Mexican drug cartels to target and assassinate the journalist Griselda Triana after her husband Javier Valdez Cárdenas, also an investigative reporter, was assassinated in 2017. The Mexican government is also directly implicated in targeting journalists and civil society members with Pegasus spyware, according to research and analysis by Canada's Citizen Lab.[117]

After the reporter Jamal Khashoggi was killed and dismembered at the Saudi consulate in Istanbul in October 2018, it was discovered that an NSO client targeted the phone of his fiancée, Hanan Elatr.[118] Pegasus transforms a cellular phone into a mobile surveillance device, activating microphones and cameras without the user's knowledge.

Skunk water, a putrid-smelling liquid, was tested and perfected on Palestinians, often with Israeli film crews recording the attacks to show potential clients the effectiveness of the chemical.[119]

"Israeli forces routinely douse entire Palestinian neighborhoods in skunk water, deliberately spraying it into private homes, businesses, schools, and funerals in what the Israeli human rights group B'Tselem calls 'a collective punitive measure' against Palestinian villages that engage in protest against Israel's colonial violence," *The Electronic Intifada* reported in 2015.[120]

That same year, the St. Louis Metropolitan Police Department purchased fourteen canisters of skunk to use against protesters following demonstrations that erupted after the police killing of unarmed African-American teenager Michael Brown in Ferguson, Missouri.[121]

Israel created a sophisticated facial recognition system, Red Wolf, to document every Palestinian in the occupied territories. The technology "is used extensively" to "consolidate existing practices of discriminatory policing, segregation, and curbing freedom of movement, violating Palestinians' basic rights," Amnesty International explains in its May 2023 report titled "Automated Apartheid."[122] The French investigative outlet *Disclose* revealed that French police have been unlawfully using facial recognition software provided by the Israeli technology firm, BriefCam, for eight years. BriefCam's technology allows users to "detect, track, extract, classify, [and] catalog" people "appearing in video surveillance footage in real-time."[123]

AI-machine guns, manufactured by the Israeli company SMARTSHOOTER, can fire stun grenades and sponge-tipped bullets as well as tear gas. They were perfected in trials on the Palestinians in the West Bank. SMARTSHOOTER was recently awarded a contract to supply the British Army with its SMASH "automatic targeting and firing system" which can be attached to small arms such as automatic rifles.

Israel, according to Jeff Halper in his book *War Against the People*, has done cutting-edge work on cyborg soldiers. Israel also developed a radar system that sees through walls, he writes.[124] As *The Electronic Intifada* explains, Israel's military-industrial complex has built "a tank named Cruelty, a twenty-gram drone in the shape of a butterfly, a stealth 'wonder boat' called the Death Shark, a series of weapons named after insects or natural phenomena (bionic hornets, smart dust, dragonfly drones and smart dew robots), cybernetic insects, a six-hundred-building 'urban warfare' training center nicknamed Chicago and a one-megaton bomb containing electromagnetic pulse capability."[125]

Halper notes that during the occupation of Iraq, the US military replicated the tactics used by Israel against the Palestinians. It constructed a security barrier around the Baghdad Green Zone, imposed closures on towns and villages, carried out targeted assassinations, copied Israeli torture techniques, and used checkpoints and roadblocks to isolate towns and villages.

Israel trains and equips US police forces, teaching aggressive tactics backed up by heavy military hardware and vehicles, which were used in Ferguson and Atlanta during the police confrontations with activists who were protesting Atlanta Public Safety Training Center (Cop City).

Halper calls this the "Palestinianization" of global conflicts.

"With so many Israeli companies involved in maintaining the infrastructure around the occupation, these firms found innovative ways to sell their services to the state, test the latest technology on Palestinians, and then promote them around the world," Loewenstein explains. And while "the defense industries are increasingly in private hands," following decades of neoliberal privatization, "they continue to act as an extension of Israel's foreign policy agenda, supporting its goals and pro-occupation ideology."[126]

# VIII

# ZIONISM IS RACISM

I was a friend of Alina Margolis-Edelman, who was part of the armed resistance in the Warsaw Ghetto Uprising in World War II. Her husband, Marek Edelman, was the deputy commander of the uprising and the only leader to survive the war. The Nazis had sealed 400,000 Polish Jews inside the Warsaw Ghetto. The trapped Jews died in the thousands from starvation, disease, and indiscriminate violence. When the Nazis began to transport the remaining Jews to the extermination camps, the resistance fighters fought back. None expected to survive.

After the war, Marek Edelman condemned Zionism as a racist ideology used to justify the theft of Palestinian land. He sided with the Palestinians, supported their armed resistance, and met frequently with Palestinian leaders. He thundered against Israel's appropriation of the Holocaust to justify its repression of the Palestinian people. While Israel dined out on the mythology of the ghetto uprising, it treated the only surviving leader of the uprising, who refused to leave Poland, as a pariah. Edelman understood that the lesson of the Holocaust and the ghetto uprising was not that Jews are morally superior or eternal victims. History, Edelman said, belongs to everyone. The oppressed, including the Palestinians, had a right to fight for equality, dignity, and liberty.

"To be a Jew means always being with the oppressed and never the oppressors," Edelman said.[127]

The Warsaw Uprising has long inspired the Palestinians. Representatives of the PLO used to lay a wreath at the annual commemoration of the uprising in Poland at the Warsaw Ghetto monument.

The more violence the colonizer expends to subdue the occupied, the more it transforms itself into a monster. This is as true in Gaza as it was in Warsaw.

Rashid Khalidi, the Edward Said Professor of Modern Arab Studies at Columbia University, meticulously researched the long history of colonization in Palestine. His book, *The Hundred Years' War on Palestine: A History of Settler Colonization and Resistance, 1917-2017*, which includes private, internal communications between the early Zionists and Israeli leadership, leaves no doubt that the Jewish colonizers were acutely aware from the start that the Palestinian people had to be subjugated and removed to create a Jewish state.[128] The Jewish leadership was also acutely aware that its intentions had to be masked behind euphemisms, the patina of Biblical legitimacy by Jews to a land that had been Muslim since the seventh century, platitudes about human and democratic rights, the supposed benefits of colonization to the colonized, and a mendacious call for democracy and peaceful coexistence with those targeted for destruction.

Zionism was birthed from the evils of anti-Semitism. It was a response to the discrimination and violence inflicted on Jews, especially during the savage pogroms in Russia and Eastern Europe in the late nineteenth and early twentieth centuries that left thousands dead. In 1896, the founder of the Zionist movement, Theodor Herzl, published *Der Judenstaat*, or *The Jewish State*, in which he warned that Jews were not safe in Europe, a warning that within a few decades proved terrifyingly prescient.

Britain's support of a Jewish homeland was always colored by anti-Semitism. The 1917 decision by "His Majesty's Government," as stated in the Balfour Declaration, to support "the establishment in Palestine of a national home for the Jewish people" was a principal part of a misguided endeavor based on anti-Semitic tropes. It was undertaken by the ruling British elites to unite "international Jewry"—including officials of Jewish descent in senior positions in the new Bolshevik state in Russia—behind Britain's flagging military campaign in World War I.

The British leaders were convinced that Jews secretly controlled the US financial system. They thought that once promised a homeland in Palestine, American Jews would bring the United States into the war and help finance the war effort. To add to these bizarre anti-Semitic canards, the British believed that Jews and Dönme—or "crypto-Jews" whose ancestors had converted to Christianity but who continued to practice the rituals of Judaism in secret—controlled the Turkish government. If the Zionists were given a homeland in Palestine, the British believed, the Jews and Dönme would turn on the Turkish regime, which was allied with Germany in the war, and the Turkish government would collapse. World Jewry, the British were convinced, was the key to winning the war.

"With 'Great Jewry' against us," warned Britain's Sir Mark Sykes—who, with the French diplomat François Georges-Picot, created the secret treaty called the Sykes-Picot Agreement which carved up the Ottoman Empire between Britain and France—there would be no possibility of victory. Zionism, Sykes said, was a powerful global subterranean force that was "atmospheric, international, cosmopolitan, subconscious, and unwritten, nay often unspoken."[129]

The British elites, including Foreign Secretary Arthur Balfour, also believed that Jews could never be assimilated in British society and it was better for them to emigrate. Notably, the only Jewish member of Prime Minister David Lloyd George's cabinet, Edwin Montagu, vehemently opposed Zionism and the Balfour Declaration. He argued that "there is not a Jewish nation" and that it "is no more true to say that a Jewish Englishman and a Jewish Moor are of the same nation than it is to say that a Christian Englishman and a Christian Frenchman are of the same nation." A Jewish state in Palestine would, he believed, encourage states to expel its Jews. "Palestine will become the world's ghetto," Montagu warned.[130]

Montagu was proven correct after World War II when hundreds of thousands of Jewish refugees were rendered stateless. Their communities had been destroyed during the war. Their homes and land were confiscated. Survivors who returned to countries like Poland not only found that they had nowhere to live, but were often victims of discrimination as well as postwar anti-Semitic attacks and massacres. In one of the cruel ironies of history, Palestinians would experience a similar dispossession and discrimination at the hands of Zionists.

The European powers dealt with the Jewish refugee crisis by shipping victims of the Holocaust to the Middle East. So, while leading Zionists understood that they had to uproot and displace Arabs to establish a homeland, they were also acutely aware that they were not wanted in the countries from which they had fled or been expelled. The Zionists and their supporters may have mouthed slogans such as "a land without a people for a people without a land" in speaking of Palestine, but, as Hannah Arendt observed, European powers were attempting to deal with the crime carried out against Jews in Europe by committing another crime against Palestinians. It was a recipe for endless conflict.

Ze'ev Jabotinsky was the Russian father of the fascistic wing of Zionism—Revisionist Zionism—which has dominated Israel since 1977. Revisionist Zionism has been embraced by Prime Ministers Menachem Begin, Yitzhak Shamir, Ariel Sharon, Ehud Olmert, and Benjamin Netanyahu. In his 1923 essay "The Iron Wall," Jabotinsky wrote bluntly, "Every native population in the world resists colonists as long as it has the slightest hope of being able to rid itself of the danger of being colonized. That is what the Arabs in Palestine are doing, and what they will persist in doing

ZIONISM IS RACISM 103

as long as there remains a solitary spark of hope that they will be able to prevent the transformation of 'Palestine' into the 'Land of Israel.'"[131]

This kind of public honesty, Khalidi notes, was rare among leading Zionists. Most of the Zionist leaders "protested the innocent purity of their aims and deceived their Western listeners, and perhaps themselves, with fairy tales about their benign intentions toward the Arab inhabitants of Palestine," he writes.[132] The Zionists—in a situation similar to that of today's supporters of Israel—were aware it would be fatal to acknowledge that the creation of a Jewish homeland required the expulsion of the Arab majority. Such an admission would cause the colonizers to lose the world's sympathy. But among themselves, the Zionists clearly understood that the use of armed force against the Arab majority was essential for the colonial project to succeed.

"Zionist colonization . . . can proceed and develop only under the protection of a power that is independent of the native population—behind an iron wall, which the native population cannot breach," Jabotinsky wrote.[133]

The Jewish colonizers needed an imperial patron. Their first was Britain, which took control of Palestine during World War I and deployed 100,000 troops to crush the Palestinian revolt of the 1930s. Britain armed and trained Jewish militias known as the Haganah. The brutal suppression of the Arab revolt included wholesale executions and aerial bombardment and left ten percent of the adult male population dead, wounded, imprisoned, or exiled. The Zionists' second patron became the United States. Israel, despite the myth of self-reliance, would not be able to maintain its colonies without its imperial benefactors. This is why the Boycott, Divestment, and Sanctions movement is threatening.

The early Zionists bought up huge tracts of fertile Palestinian land and drove out the indigenous inhabitants. They subsidized European Jewish settlers sent to Palestine, where ninety-four percent of the inhabitants were Arabs. They created organizations such as the Jewish Colonization Association, later called the Palestine Jewish Colonization Association, to administer the Zionist project.

But, as Khalidi writes, "once colonialism took on a bad odor in the post-World War II era of decolonization, the colonial origins and practice of Zionism and Israel were whitewashed and conveniently forgotten in Israel and the West. In fact, Zionism— for two decades the coddled step-child of British colonialism— rebranded itself as an anticolonial movement."[134]

"Today, the conflict that was engendered by this classic nineteenth-century European colonial venture in a non-European land, supported from 1917 onward by the greatest Western imperial power of its age, is rarely described in such unvarnished terms," Khalidi writes. "Indeed, those who analyze not only Israeli settlement efforts in Jerusalem, the West Bank, and the occupied Syrian Golan Heights, but the entire Zionist enterprise from the perspective of its colonial-settler origins and nature are often vilified. Many cannot accept the contradiction inherent in the idea that although Zionism undoubtedly succeeded in creating a thriving national entity in Israel, its roots are as a colonial settler project (as are those of other modern countries: the United States, Canada, Australia, and New Zealand). Nor can they accept that it would not have succeeded but for the support of the great imperial powers, Britain and later the United States. Zionism, therefore, could be and was both a national and a colonial settler movement at one and the same time."[135]

During the British control of Palestine, the population was officially divided between Jews and "non-Jews." "[T]here were no such thing as Palestinians . . . they did not exist," Israeli Prime Minister Golda Meir quipped.[136] This erasure, which requires an egregious act of historical amnesia, is what the Israeli sociologist Baruch Kimmerling called the "politicide" of the Palestinian people. Khalidi writes, "The surest way to eradicate a people's right to their land is to deny their historical connection to it."[137]

The creation of the state of Israel on May 15, 1948, was achieved by the Haganah and other armed Jewish groups through the ethnic cleansing of the Palestinians and massacres that spread terror among the Palestinian population. The Haganah, trained and armed by the British, seized most of Palestine and emptied West Jerusalem and cities such as Haifa and Jaffa, along with numerous towns and villages, of their Arab inhabitants.

Since 1948, Palestinians have mounted one resistance effort after another, all unleashing disproportionate Israeli reprisals. This resistance has forced the world to recognize the presence of Palestinians, despite the feverish efforts of Israel, the United States, and many Arab regimes to remove them from historical consciousness. The repeated revolts, as Edward Said noted, gave the Palestinians the right to tell their own story, the "permission to narrate."

The colonial project has poisoned Israel, as feared by its most prescient leaders, including Moshe Dayan and Yitzhak Rabin, who was assassinated by a right-wing Jewish extremist in 1995. Israel is an apartheid state that rivals and often surpasses the savagery and racism of apartheid South Africa. Its democracy—which was always exclusively for Jews—has been hijacked by extremists, including current Prime Minister Benjamin Netanyahu, Minister of Finance Bezalel Smotrich, and Minister of National Security Itamar Ben-Gvir, who have implemented racial laws that were once championed mainly by marginalized fanatics such as Meir Kahane.

The Israeli public is infected with racism. "Death to Arabs" is a popular chant at Israeli soccer matches. Jewish mobs and vigilantes, including thugs from right-wing youth groups such as Im Tirtzu, carry out indiscriminate acts of vandalism and violence against dissidents, Palestinians, Israeli Arabs, and the hapless African immigrants who live crammed into the slums of Tel Aviv. Israel has promulgated a series of discriminatory laws against non-Jews that resemble the racist Nuremberg Laws that disenfranchised Jews in Nazi Germany. The Communities Acceptance Law permits exclusively Jewish towns in Israel's Galilee region to bar applicants for residency on the basis of "suitability to the community's fundamental outlook." Uri Avnery warned that "Israel's very existence is threatened by fascism."[138]

In recent years, up to one million Israelis have left to live in the United States and elsewhere, many of them among Israel's most enlightened and educated citizens. From October 7, 2023, until the end of that month, 370,000 Israelis left, and a further 139,839 left the following month.[139]

Within Israel, human rights campaigners, intellectuals, and journalists—both Israeli and Palestinian—have found themselves vilified as traitors in government-sponsored smear campaigns, placed under state surveillance, and subjected to arbitrary arrests. The Israeli educational system, starting in primary school, is an indoctrination machine for the military. Israel runs the Saharonim detention camp in the Negev Desert, one of the largest detention centers in the world, where African immigrants can be held for up to three years without trial. Also in the Negev is the notorious Sde Teiman camp where following October 7, 2023, Israelis detained thousands of Palestinians from Gaza as "unlawful combatants" without charges. They are denied basic human rights, including access to lawyers. Following whistleblowing by employees who worked at the camp and testimonies by released prisoners, it was revealed prisoners at this camp were regularly beaten and tortured, with at least thirty-five Palestinians tortured to death.[140]

Fadi Baker, a twenty-five-year-old lawyer specializing in human rights, from the Tel Al-Hawa neighborhood in Gaza City, gave his account over the phone of the torture he endured to B'Tselem field researcher Olfat Al-Kurd, on June 23, 2024.[141]

On January 5, 2024, while out searching for flour to feed his family, Baker explains, Israeli soldiers shot him in the leg and lower abdomen. Hours later other Israeli soldiers found him.

"They stripped me naked and took the gold jewelry, my money, and my phone. Another soldier came and handed me a phone. I talked to someone who asked me in Arabic which tunnel I'd come out of. I told him I was a civilian and hadn't come out of any tunnel. Then he told me he would meet me and suggested I didn't talk to the soldiers in the meantime because they would kill me."[142]

He was then blindfolded, tied, and driven in an army truck to another location as his head banged against the truck. After the truck stopped and he was cut free, he fell to the ground and was taken to be interrogated.

He was beaten and later told to put on "white see-through clothes." Baker was robbed of his belongings and tortured. He was taken to the Sde Teiman detention facility, where Israelis wearing medical and military uniforms cauterized his wounds without anesthetic. He was photographed. His belongings were taken from him. He was later forced into something "that looked like an animal pen." He was forced to kneel, kept blindfolded and handcuffed, and not permitted to sleep. Five days later he was taken to a "very cold room," stripped naked, and left for four days while loud music was blasted into the room day and night.

He goes on:

> After four days, they took me for interrogation, which was based on beatings and torture. They put cigarettes out in my mouth and on my body. They put clamps on my testicles that were attached to something heavy. It went on like that for a whole day. My testicles swelled up and my left ear bled. I was asked about Hamas leaders and people I didn't know and hadn't met. They asked me where I was on 7 October, and I said I was at home and had only gone out to get food for my wife. They beat me. Then they put me back in the

freezing room with the loud disco music, and again left me there, naked, for two days, and gave me only very little bread and water.

Then they took me into interrogation again. They opened WhatsApp on my phone and asked me about neighbors from my building and where they worked. I told them that some of them worked at UNRWA or the Red Cross and some I didn't know.

From there, they took me to a different pen, where they left me naked for about four or five days. I got very little food and drink there too, and they made me wear a diaper. After that, I was taken into interrogation again. I was asked about my work and about car dealers I have business connections with. During the interrogation, they showed me a video and told me they were Islamic Jihad people. I told them I didn't know them. During the interrogation, I was given electric shocks and beaten so badly that I passed out. My foot got swollen from the electric shocks. When I came to, I asked them to bandage it and they did. The interrogation continued, and then they took me back to the room with the disco [music] and left me there for three days. When I asked the soldier guarding me to go to the bathroom, he brought me a container and told me to pee into it. I developed wounds, bleeding and pain in my body, especially the left leg, which had bruises and wounds full of pus that hurt badly. My leg turned blue and nearly reached a state of necrosis.

I was kept in the pen for five days, and then I had surgery, without anesthesia, on my swollen left leg. I asked for anesthetics and they said I wasn't in a position to ask for anything and ordered me to keep quiet. When I screamed in pain, they hit me in the abdomen with a plastic stick until I shut up. They drained the pus from my leg.

Then they moved me back to the pen, where I was forced to kneel every day for two weeks, handcuffed and blind-folded. We got food three times a day—cheese, jam, tuna, and four slices of bread. The bandage on my leg was changed only once. We showered once a week and got clean under-wear only once during that time.

I was offered to work with the army and refused. One of the officers or soldiers conveyed condolences for the death of my father and mother, my family and my wife. That's when I had a nervous breakdown and I passed out.[143]

On February 25, 2024, at 3 a.m., Baker was put on a bus with other detainees and driven to the Karam Abu Salem (Kerem Shalom) crossing into Gaza. He and the other detainees were told by the soldiers they were forbidden to speak to the media about what they had endured.

"They gave us a bag with our personal effects, but I didn't find the money, the gold jewelry, or my phone in mine," he said. "I only found the phone charger, my UNRWA refugee card, and my ID card. I told the soldier I wanted my things, and he said I had nothing and that if I spoke about it, I would go back to prison."[144]

While Baker was detained, his wife, badly malnourished, gave birth to their first child, a girl. His daughter weighed nearly four and a half pounds when she was born. His father and mother, he later discovered, were also still alive.

The Jewish scholar Yeshayahu Leibowitz, whom Isaiah Berlin called "the conscience of Israel," saw the mortal danger to Israel of its colonial project. He warned that if Israel did not separate church and state and end its colonial occupation, it would give rise to a corrupt Rabbinate that would warp Judaism into a fascistic cult. "Religious nationalism is to religion what National Socialism was to socialism," said Leibowitz, who died in 1994.[145] He saw that the blind veneration of the military, especially after the 1967 war, would result in the degeneration of the Jewish society and the death of democracy.

"[O]ur situation will deteriorate to that of a second Vietnam [a reference to the war waged by the United States in the 1970s], to a war in constant escalation without prospect of ultimate resolution," Leibowitz wrote.[146] He foresaw that "the Arabs would be the working people and the Jews the administrators, inspectors, officials, and police—mainly secret police. A state ruling a hostile population of 1.5 million to 2 million foreigners would necessarily become a secret-police state, with all that this implies for education, free speech, and democratic institutions. The corruption characteristic of every colonial regime would also prevail in the State of Israel. The administration would have to suppress Arab insurgency on the one hand and acquire Arab Quislings on the other. There is also good reason to fear that the Israel Defense Forces, which has been until now a people's army, would, as a result of being transformed into an army of occupation, degenerate, and its commanders, who will have become military governors, resemble their colleagues in other nations."[147]

Israel has dropped its rhetoric about peace, democracy, and rights. Its sadistic manipulation of the Palestinians is transparent.

*Run, the Israelis demand of the Palestinians in Gaza, run for your lives. Run from Rafah the way you ran from Gaza City, the way you ran from Jabaliya, the way you ran from Deir Al-Balah, the way you ran from Beit Hanoun, the way you ran from Bani Suheila, the way you ran from Khan Yunis. Run or we will kill you. We will drop GBU-39 bombs on your tent encampments and set them ablaze. We will spray you with bullets from our machine-gun-equipped drones. We will pound you with artillery and tank shells. We will shoot you down with snipers. We will decimate your tents, your refugee camps, your cities and towns, your homes, your schools, your hospitals, and your water purification plants. We will rain death from the sky.*

*Run for your lives. Again and again and again. Pack up the few belongings you have left. Blankets. A couple of pots. Some clothes. We don't care how exhausted you are, how hungry you are, how terrified you are, how sick you are, how old, or how young you are. Run. Run. Run. And when you run in terror to one part of Gaza, we will make you turn around and run to another. Trapped in a labyrinth of death. Back and forth. Up and down. Side to side. Six. Seven. Eight times. We toy with you like mice in a trap. Then we deport you, so you can never return. Or we kill you.*

*Let the world denounce our genocide. What do we care? The billions in military aid flows unchecked from our American ally. The fighter jets. The artillery shells. The tanks. The bombs. An endless supply. We kill children by the thousands. We kill women and the elderly by the thousands. The sick and injured, without medicine and hospitals, die. We poison the water. We cut off the food. We make you starve. We created this hell. We are the masters. Law. Duty. A code of conduct. They do not exist for us. But first we toy with you. We humiliate you. We terrorize you. We revel in your fear. We are amused by your pathetic attempts to survive. You are not human. You are creatures. Untermensch. We feed our lust for domination. Look at our posts on social media. They have gone viral. One shows soldiers grinning in a Palestinian home with the owners tied up and blindfolded in the background. We loot. Rugs. Cosmetics. Motorbikes. Jewelry. Watches. Cash. Gold. Antiquities. We mock your misery. We cheer your death. We celebrate our religion, our nation, our identity, our superiority, by negating and erasing yours.*

*Depravity is moral. Atrocity is heroism. Genocide is redemption.*

This is the game of terror played by Israel in Gaza. It was the game played during the Dirty War in Argentina when the military junta "disappeared" thirty thousand of its own citizens. The "disappeared" were subjected to torture—as are Palestinians in Israeli prisons—and humiliated before they were murdered. It was the game played in the clandestine torture centers and prisons in El Salvador and Iraq. It is what characterized the war in Bosnia in the Serbian concentration camps.

Israeli journalist Yinon Magal, on the show *Hapatriotim* on Israel's *Channel 14*, joked that Joe Biden's red line was the killing of thirty thousand Palestinians. The singer Kobi Peretz asked if that was the number of dead for a day. The audience erupted in applause and laughter.

We know Israel's intent.

We cannot plead ignorance.

But it is easier to pretend. Pretend Israel will allow humanitarian aid. Pretend there will be a permanent ceasefire. Pretend Palestinians will return to their destroyed homes. Pretend Gaza will be rebuilt—the hospitals, the universities, the mosques, the housing. Pretend the Palestinian Authority will administer Gaza. Pretend there will be a two-state solution. Pretend there is no genocide.

We do not halt Israel's genocide because we, as Americans, are Israel, infected with the same white supremacy, the same settler-colonial roots. We are intoxicated by our domination of the globe's wealth and the power to obliterate others with our advanced weaponry.

"Mockery of every sort was added to their deaths," the Roman historian Tacitus wrote of those the emperor Nero singled out for torture and death. "Covered with the skins of beasts, they were torn by dogs and perished, or were nailed to crosses, or were doomed to the flames and burnt, to serve as a nightly illumination, when daylight had expired."[148]

Sadism by the powerful is the curse of the human condition. It was as prevalent in ancient Rome as it is in Gaza.

We know the modern face of Nero, who illuminated his opulent garden parties by burning to death captives tied to stakes. That is not in dispute.

But who were Nero's guests? Who wandered through the emperor's grounds, as human beings—as in Rafah—were burned alive? How could these guests see, and no doubt hear, such horrendous suffering and witness such appalling torture and be indifferent, even content?

We are Nero's guests.[149]

The Palestinians have long been betrayed, not only by us in the Global North, but by most of the governments in the Muslim world. We stand passive in the face of the crime of crimes. History will judge Israel for this genocide. But it will also judge us. It will ask why we did not do more, why we did not sever all agreements, all trade deals, all accords, and all cooperation with the apartheid state, why we did not halt weapons shipments to Israel, why we did not recall our ambassadors, why when the maritime trade in the Red Sea was disrupted by Yemen, an alternative overland route into Israel was set up by Saudi Arabia, United Arab Emirates, and Jordan, and why we did not do everything in our power to end the slaughter.

The opposite of good is not evil, as Rabbi Abraham Joshua Heschel cautioned. The opposite of good is indifference.[150]

The Palestinian resistance is our resistance. The Palestinian struggle for dignity, freedom, and independence is our struggle. The Palestinian cause is our cause. For, as history has also shown, those who were once Nero's guests, soon became Nero's victims.

IX.

# DIVINE VIOLENCE

November 2023: I am in the studio of *Al Jazeera*'s Arabic channel in Doha, Qatar, watching a live feed from Gaza City. The *Al Jazeera* reporter in northern Gaza, because of the intense Israeli shelling, was forced to evacuate to southern Gaza. He left his camera behind. He trained it on Al-Shifa Hospital, Gaza's largest medical complex. It is night. Israeli tanks fire directly towards the hospital compound. Long horizontal red flashes. A deliberate attack on a hospital. A deliberate war crime. A deliberate massacre of the most helpless civilians, including the very sick and infants. Then the feed goes dead.

We sit in front of the monitors. We are silent. We know what this means. No power. No water. No internet. No medical supplies. Every infant in an incubator will die. Every dialysis patient will die. Everyone in the intensive care unit will die. Everyone who needs oxygen will die. Everyone who needs emergency surgery will die. And what will happen to the fifty thousand people who, driven from their homes by the relentless bombing, have taken refuge on the hospital grounds? We know the answer to that as well. Many of them, too, will die.

Israel blames Hamas and the Palestinians for its war crimes. It insists that hospitals are Hamas command centers and legitimate targets. Israel rarely provides evidence.

Médecins Sans Frontières (MSF), which had staff working in Al-Shifa Hospital, issued a statement during the siege of the hospital saying patients, doctors, and nurses are "trapped in hospitals under fire." It called on the "Israeli government to cease this unrelenting assault on Gaza's health system."

"Over the past twenty-four hours, hospitals in Gaza have been under relentless bombardment. Al-Shifa Hospital complex, the biggest health facility where MSF staff are still working, has been hit several times, including the maternity and outpatient departments, resulting in multiple deaths and injuries," the statement read. "The hostilities around the hospital have not stopped. MSF teams and hundreds of patients are still inside Al-Shifa Hospital. MSF urgently reiterates its calls to stop the attacks against hospitals, for an immediate ceasefire and for the protection of medical facilities, medical staff, and patients."[151]

Three other hospitals in northern Gaza and Gaza City were also encircled by Israeli forces and tanks in what a doctor told *Al Jazeera* was a "day of war against hospitals." The Indonesian Hospital lost power. As of September 12, 2024, "only seventeen of thirty-six hospitals remain partially functional in Gaza," according to the World Health Organization which also noted that, "while primary health care and community-level services are frequently suspended or rendered inaccessible due to insecurity, attacks, and repeated evacuation orders."[152]

If you were a Palestinian in Gaza and had access to a weapon, what would you do? If Israel killed your family and reduced your neighborhood to rubble, how would you react? Why would you care about international or humanitarian law when you know it only applies to the oppressed, not the oppressors? If terror is the only language Israel uses to communicate, the only language it apparently understands, wouldn't you speak back with terror? Is extremism the answer to extremism? Does mass slaughter and genocide require those who resist to forfeit their own lives?

When twenty-five-year-old Aaron Bushnell placed his cell phone on the ground to set up a live stream and lit himself on fire in front of the Israeli embassy in Washington D.C., resulting in his death, he pitted divine violence against radical evil. As an active-duty member of the US Air Force, he was part of the vast machinery that sustains the ongoing genocide in Gaza, no less morally culpable than the German soldiers, technocrats, engineers, scientists, and bureaucrats who oiled the apparatus of the Nazi Holocaust. This was a role he could no longer accept.

He died for our sins.

"I will no longer be complicit in genocide," he said calmly in his video as he walked to the gate of the embassy. "I am about to engage in an extreme act of protest. But compared to what people have been experiencing in Palestine at the hands of their colonizers, it's not extreme at all. This is what our ruling class has decided will be normal."[153]

Young men and women sign up for the military for many reasons, but starving, bombing, and killing women and children is usually not amongst them. Shouldn't, in a just world, the US fleet break the Israeli blockade of Gaza to provide food, shelter, and medicine? Shouldn't US warplanes impose a no-fly zone over Gaza to halt the saturation bombing? Shouldn't Israel be issued an ultimatum to withdraw its forces from Gaza? Shouldn't the weapons shipments, billions in military aid and intelligence provided to Israel, be halted? Shouldn't those who commit genocide, as well as those who support genocide, be held accountable?

These simple questions are the ones Bushnell's death forces us to confront.

"Many of us like to ask ourselves," he posted shortly before his suicide, "'What would I do if I was alive during slavery? Or the Jim Crow South? Or apartheid? What would I do if my country was committing genocide?' The answer is, you're doing it. Right now."

The coalition forces intervened in northern Iraq in 1991 to protect the Kurds following the first Gulf War. The suffering of the Kurds was extensive but dwarfed by the genocide in Gaza. A no-fly zone for the Iraqi air force was imposed. The Iraqi military was pushed out of the northern Kurdish areas. Humanitarian aid saved Kurds from starvation, infectious diseases, and death from exposure.

But that was another time, another war. Genocide is evil when it is carried out by our enemies. It is defended and sustained when carried out by our allies.

In his essay "Critique of Violence," Walter Benjamin—whose friends Christoph "Fritz" Heinle and Friederike (Rika) Seligson committed suicide in 1914 to protest German militarism during World War I—examines acts of violence undertaken by individuals who confront radical evil.[154] Any act that defies radical evil breaks the law in the name of justice. It affirms the sovereignty and dignity of the individual. It condemns the coercive violence of the state. It entails a willingness to die. Benjamin called these extreme acts of resistance "divine violence."[155]

"Only for the sake of the hopeless ones have we been given hope,"[156] Benjamin writes.

Israel's *lebensraum* master plan for Gaza, borrowed from the Nazi's depopulation of Jewish ghettos, is clear. Turn Gaza into a mortuary.

The Nazis shipped their victims to death camps. The Israelis seek to ship their victims to squalid refugee camps in countries outside of Israel.

This is the plan. No one in Washington intends to stop it.

We all have the capacity, with little prodding, to become willing executioners. The line between the victim and the victimizer is razor-thin. The dark lusts of racial and ethnic supremacy, of vengeance and hate, of the eradication of those we condemn as embodying evil, are poisons that are not circumscribed by race, nationality, ethnicity, or religion. We can all become Nazis. It takes very little. And if we do not stand in eternal vigilance over evil—our evil—we become, like those carrying out the mass killing in Gaza, monsters.

The cries of those expiring under the rubble in Gaza are the cries of the over 1.5 million Cambodians killed by the Khmer Rouge, the thousands of Tutsi families burned alive in churches, and the tens of thousands of Jews executed by the Einsatzgruppen at Babi Yar in Ukraine. The Holocaust is not a historical relic. It lives, lurking in the shadows, waiting to ignite its vicious contagion.

We were warned. Raul Hilberg. Primo Levi. Bruno Bettelheim. Hannah Arendt. Aleksandr Solzhenitsyn. They understood the dark recesses of the human spirit. But this truth is bitter and hard to confront. We prefer the myth. We prefer to see in our own kind, our own race, our own ethnicity, our own nation, our own religion, superior virtues. We prefer to sanctify our hatred.

Some of those who bore witness to this awful truth—including Jean Améry, the author of *At the Mind's Limits: Contemplations by a Survivor on Auschwitz and Its Realities,* and Tadeusz Borowski, who wrote *This Way for the Gas, Ladies and Gentlemen*—committed suicide. The German playwright and revolutionary Ernst Toller, unable to rouse an indifferent world to assist victims and refugees from the Spanish Civil War, hanged himself in 1939 in a room at the Mayflower Hotel in New York City. On his hotel desk were photos of dead Spanish children.

Hilberg, in his monumental work *The Destruction of the European Jews*, chronicled a process of repression that at first was "relatively mild," but led, step by step, to the Holocaust. It started with legal discrimination and ended with mass murder. "[T]he destructive process was a development that was begun with caution and ended without restraint," he wrote.[57]

The Palestinians have endured a similar "destructive process." They have gradually been stripped of basic civil liberties; robbed of assets, including much of their land and often their homes;

have suffered from mounting restrictions on their physical movements; been blocked from trading and business, especially the selling of produce; and found themselves increasingly impoverished and finally trapped behind walls and security fences erected around Gaza and the West Bank.

"The process of destruction [of the European Jews] unfolded in a definite pattern," Hilberg wrote. "It did not, however, proceed from a basic plan. No bureaucrat in 1933 could have predicted what kind of measures would be taken in 1938, nor was it possible in 1938 to foretell the configuration of the undertaking in 1942. The destructive process was a step-by-step operation, and the administrator could seldom see more than one step ahead."[158]

There may not be transports or extermination camps for the Palestinians—although the killing fields of Gaza are clearly genocidal—but amid increasing violence against Palestinians, larger and larger numbers of them will die from airstrikes, targeted assassinations, starvation, and disease. Hunger and misery will continue to expand. Israeli demands for "transfer"—the forced expulsion of Palestinians from occupied territory to neighboring countries—will continue to grow.

The belief that a race or class is contaminated is used by ruling elites to justify quarantining the people of that group. But quarantine is only the first step. The despised group can never be redeemed or cured—Hannah Arendt noted that all racists see such contamination as something that can never be eradicated. The fear of the other is stoked by racist leaders such as Netanyahu, to create permanent instability. This instability is exploited by a corrupt power elite that is also seeking the destruction of civil society.

Primo Levi railed against the false, morally uplifting narrative of the Holocaust that culminates in the creation of the state of Israel, a narrative embraced by the Holocaust Museum in Washington, D.C. The contemporary history of the Third Reich, he writes, could be "reread as a war against memory, an Orwellian falsification of memory, falsification of reality, negation of reality."[159] He wonders if "we who have returned" have "been able to understand and make others understand our experience."[160]

Levi saw us reflected in Chaim Rumkowski, the Nazi collaborator and tyrannical leader of the Łódź Ghetto. Rumkowski sold out his fellow Jews for privilege and power, although he was sent to Auschwitz on the final transport where Jewish *Sonderkommando*—prisoners forced to help herd victims into the gas chambers and dispose of their bodies—in an act of vengeance, reportedly beat him to death outside a crematorium.

"We are all mirrored in Rumkowski," Levi reminds us. "His ambiguity is ours, it is our second nature, we hybrids molded from clay and spirit. His fever is ours, the fever of Western civilization, that 'descends into hell with trumpets and drums,' and its miserable adornments are the distorting image of our symbols of social prestige." We, like Rumkowski, "are so dazzled by power and prestige as to forget our essential fragility. Willingly or not we come to terms with power, forgetting that we are all in the ghetto, that the ghetto is walled in, that outside the ghetto reign the lords of death, and that close by the train is waiting."[161]

Levi insists that the camps "could not be reduced to the two blocks of victims and persecutors."[162] He argues, "It is naive, absurd, and historically false to believe that an infernal system such as National Socialism sanctifies its victims; on the contrary; it degrades them, it makes them resemble itself."[163] He chronicles what he called the "gray zone" between corruption and collaboration. The world, he writes, is not black and white, "but a vast zone of gray consciences that stands between the great men of evil and the pure victims."[164] We all inhabit this gray zone. We all can be induced to become part of the apparatus of death for trivial reasons and paltry rewards. This is the terrifying truth of the Holocaust.

It is hard not to be cynical about the plethora of university courses about the Holocaust given the censorship and banning of groups such as Students for Justice in Palestine and Jewish Voice for Peace, imposed by university administrations. It is hard not to be cynical about the "humanitarian interventionists"—Barack Obama, Tony Blair, Boris Johnson, Hillary Clinton, Joe Biden—who talk in sanctimonious rhymes about the "Responsibility to Protect" but are silent about war crimes when speaking out would threaten their status and careers. None of the "humanitarian interventions" they champion, from Bosnia to Ukraine, come close to replicating the suffering and slaughter in Gaza. But there is a cost to defending Palestinians that they do not intend to pay. There is nothing moral about denouncing slavery, the Holocaust, or dictatorial regimes that oppose the United States. All it means is you champion the dominant narrative.

The moral universe has been turned upside down. Those who oppose genocide are accused of advocating it. Those who carry out genocide are said to have the right to "defend" themselves. Vetoing ceasefires and providing two-thousand-pound bombs to Israel that throw out metal fragments thousands of feet is the road to peace. Refusing to negotiate with Hamas will save the hostages. Bombing hospitals, schools, mosques, churches, ambulances, and refugee camps, along with killing three Israeli hostages in Gaza, stripped to the waist, waving improvised white flags, and calling out for help in Hebrew, are routine acts of war. None of this makes sense, as protesters around the world realize.

"I fear that we live in a world in which war and racism are ubiquitous, in which the powers of government mobilization and legitimization are powerful and increasing, in which a sense of personal responsibility is increasingly attenuated by specialization and bureaucratization, and in which the peer group exerts tremendous pressures on behavior and sets moral norms," Christopher R. Browning writes in *Ordinary Men*, about a German reserve police battalion in World War II that was ultimately responsible for the murder of eighty-three thousand Jews. "In such a world, I fear, modern governments that wish to commit mass murder will seldom fail in their efforts for being unable to induce 'ordinary men' to become their 'willing executioners.'"[165]

Evil is protean. It mutates. It finds new forms and new expressions. Germany orchestrated the murder of six million Jews, as well as over six million Romani, Poles, homosexuals, communists, Jehovah's Witnesses, Freemasons, artists, journalists, Soviet prisoners of war, people with physical and intellectual disabilities, and political opponents. It immediately set out after the war to expiate itself for its crimes. It deftly transferred its racism and demonization to Muslims, with racial supremacy remaining firmly rooted in the German psyche. At the same time, Germany and the US rehabilitated thousands of former Nazis, especially from the intelligence services and the scientific community, and did little to prosecute those who directed Nazi war crimes. Germany today is Israel's second-largest arms supplier following the United States.

The supposed campaign against anti-Semitism, interpreted as any statement that is critical of the State of Israel or denounces the genocide, is, in fact, the championing of White power. It is why the German state, which has effectively criminalized support for the Palestinians, and the most retrograde white supremacists in the United States justify the carnage. Germany's long relationship with Israel, including paying over $90 billion since 1945 in reparations to Holocaust survivors and their heirs, is not about atonement, as Ilan Pappé explains, but blackmail.

"The argument for a Jewish state as compensation for the Holocaust was a powerful argument, so powerful that nobody listened to the outright rejection of the UN solution by the overwhelming majority of the people of Palestine," Pappé writes. "What comes out clearly is a European wish to atone. The basic and natural rights of the Palestinians should be sidelined, dwarfed and forgotten altogether for the sake of the forgiveness that Europe was seeking from the newly formed Jewish state. It was much easier to rectify the Nazi evil vis-à-vis a Zionist movement than facing the Jews of the world in general. It was less complex and, more importantly, it did not involve facing the victims of the Holocaust themselves, but rather a state that claimed to represent them. The price for this more convenient atonement was robbing the Palestinians of every basic and natural right they had and allowing the Zionist movement to ethnically cleanse them without fear of any rebuke or condemnation."[166]

The Holocaust was weaponized the moment Israel was founded. It was bastardized to serve the apartheid state.

Aaron Bushnell's self-immolation—one most social media posts and news organizations heavily censored—is the point. It is meant to be seen. Bushnell extinguished his life in the same way thousands of Palestinians, including children, have been extinguished. We could watch him burn to death. This is what it looks like. This is what happens to Palestinians because of us.

The image of Bushnell's self-immolation, like that of the Buddhist monk Thích Quảng Đức in Vietnam in 1963 or Mohamed Bouazizi, a young fruit seller in Tunisia in 2010, is a potent political message. It jolts the viewer out of somnolence. It forces the viewer to question assumptions. It begs the viewer to act. It is political theater, or perhaps religious ritual, in its most potent form. Buddhist monk Thích Nhất Hạnh said of self-immolation: "To express will by burning oneself, therefore, is not to commit an act of destruction but to perform an act of construction, that is, to suffer and to die for the sake of one's people."[167]

If Bushnell was willing to die while repeatedly shouting "Free Palestine!" as he burned, then something is terribly, terribly wrong.

These individual self-sacrifices often become rallying points for mass opposition. They can ignite—as they did in Tunisia, Libya, Egypt, Yemen, Bahrain, and Syria—revolutionary upheavals. Bouazizi, who was incensed that local authorities had confiscated his scales and produce, did not intend to start a revolution. But the petty and humiliating injustices he endured under the corrupt President Zine El-Abidine Ben Ali regime resonated with an abused public. If he could die, they could take to the streets.

These acts are sacrificial births. They presage something new. They are the complete rejection, in its most dramatic form, of conventions and reigning systems of power. They are designed to be horrific. They are meant to shock. Burning to death is one of the most dreaded ways to die.

Self-immolation comes from the Latin stem *immolāre*, to sprinkle with salted flour when offering up a consecrated victim for sacrifice. Self-immolations, like Bushnell's, link the sacred and the profane through the medium of sacrificial death.

But to go to this extreme requires what the theologian Reinhold Niebuhr calls "a sublime madness in the soul." He notes that "nothing but such madness will do battle with malignant power and spiritual wickedness in high places."[168] This madness is dangerous, but it is necessary when confronting radical evil because without it, "truth is obscured." Liberalism, Niebuhr warns, "lacks the spirit of enthusiasm, not to say fanaticism, which is so necessary to move the world out of its beaten tracks. It is too intellectual and too little emotional to be an efficient force in history."[169]

This extreme protest, this "sublime madness," has been a potent weapon in the hands of the oppressed throughout history.

The hundred and sixty self-immolations in Tibet since 2009 to protest Chinese occupation are perceived as religious rites, acts that declare the independence of the victims from the control of the state. Self-immolation calls us to a different way of being. These sacrificial victims become martyrs.

Communities of resistance, even if they are secular, are bound together by the sacrifices of martyrs. Only apostates betray their memory. The martyr, through his or her example of self-sacrifice, weakens and severs the bonds and the coercive power of the state. The martyr represents a total rejection of the status quo. This is why all states seek to discredit the martyr or turn the martyr into a nonperson. They know and fear the power of the martyr, even in death.

In 1965, Daniel Ellsberg witnessed a twenty-two-year-old anti-war activist, Norman Morrison, douse himself with kerosene and light himself on fire—the flames shot ten feet into the air outside the office of Secretary of Defense Robert McNamara at the Pentagon—to protest the Vietnam War. Ellsberg cited the self-immolation, along with the nationwide anti-war protests, as one of the factors that led him to release the Pentagon Papers.

The radical Catholic priest, Daniel Berrigan, after traveling to North Vietnam with a peace delegation during the war, visited the hospital room of Ronald Brazee. Brazee was a high school student who had drenched himself with kerosene and immolated himself outside the Cathedral of the Immaculate Conception in downtown Syracuse, New York, to protest the war.

"He was still living a month later," Berrigan writes. "I was able to gain access to him. I smelled the odor of burning flesh and I understood anew what I had seen in North Vietnam. The boy was dying in torment, his body like a great piece of meat cast upon a grill. He died shortly thereafter. I felt that my senses had been invaded in a new way. I had understood the power of death in the modern world. I knew I must speak and act against death because this boy's death was being multiplied a thousandfold in the Land of Burning Children. So I went to Catonsville because I had gone to Hanoi."[170]

In Catonsville, Maryland, Berrigan and eight other activists, known as the Catonsville Nine, broke into a draft board on May 17, 1968. They took 378 draft files and burned them with homemade napalm in the parking lot. Berrigan was sentenced to three years in a federal prison.

I was in Prague in 1989 for the Velvet Revolution. I attended the commemoration of the self-immolation of Jan Palach, a twenty-year-old university student. Palach had stood on the steps outside the National Theater in Wenceslas Square in 1969, poured petrol over himself, and lit himself on fire. He died of his wounds three days later. He left behind a note saying that this act was the only way to protest the Soviet invasion of Czechoslovakia, which had taken place five months earlier. His funeral procession was broken up by police. When frequent candlelit vigils were held at his grave at Olšany Cemetery, the communist authorities, determined to stamp out his memory, disinterred his body, cremated it, and handed the ashes to his mother.

During the winter of 1989, posters with Palach's face covered the walls of Prague. His death two decades earlier was lionized as the supreme act of resistance against the Soviets and the pro-Soviet regime installed after the overthrow of Alexander Dubček. Thousands of people marched to the Square of Red Army Soldiers and renamed it Jan Palach Square. He won.

One day, if the corporate state and apartheid state of Israel are dismantled, the street where Bushnell lit himself on fire will bear his name. He will, like Palach, be honored for his moral courage. Palestinians, betrayed by most of the world, already look to him as a hero. Palestine and Yemen have named streets after him. Because of him, it will be impossible to demonize all of us.

Divine violence terrifies a corrupt and discredited ruling class. It exposes their depravity. It illustrates that not everyone is paralyzed by fear. It is a siren call to battle radical evil. That is what Bushnell intended. His sacrifice speaks to our better selves.

# X

# THE NATION'S CONSCIENCE

May 2024: I am sitting on a fire escape across the street from Columbia University with three organizers of the Gaza encampment. It is night. New York City Police, stationed inside and outside the gates of the campus, have placed the campus on lockdown. There are barricades blocking streets. No one, unless they live in a residence hall on campus, is allowed to enter. The siege means that students cannot go to class. Students cannot go to the library. Students cannot enter the labs. Students cannot visit the university's health services. Students cannot get to studios to practice. Students cannot attend lectures. Students cannot walk across the campus lawns. The university, as during the Covid pandemic, has retreated into the world of screens where students are isolated in their rooms.

The university buildings are largely vacant. The campus pathways deserted. Columbia is a Potemkin university, a playground for corporate administrators. The president of the university—a British-Egyptian baroness who built her career at institutions such as the Bank of England, World Bank, and International Monetary Fund—called in police in riot gear, with guns drawn, to clear the school's encampment, forcibly evict students who occupied a campus hall, and beat and arrest over one hundred of them. They were arrested for "criminal trespassing" on their own campus.[171] Minouche Shafik resigned abruptly in August 2024 after enduring months of pressure from members of Congress and campus constituents over her handling of the student protests.

These administrators demand, like all who manage corporate systems of power, total obedience. Dissent. Freedom of expression. Critical thought. Moral outrage. These have no place in our corporate-indentured universities.

All systems of totalitarianism, including corporate totalitarianism, deform education into vocational training where students are taught what to think, not how to think. Only the skills and expertise demanded by the corporate state are valued. The withering away of the humanities and transformation of major research universities into corporate and Defense Department vocational schools with their outsized emphasis on business, science, technology, engineering, and math, illustrate this shift. The students who disrupt the Potemkin university, who dare to think for themselves, face beatings, suspension, arrest, and expulsion.

The mandarins who run Columbia and other universities, corporatists who make salaries in the hundreds of thousands of dollars, oversee academic plantations. They treat their poorly paid adjunct faculty, who often lack health insurance and benefits, like serfs. They slavishly serve the interests of wealthy donors and corporations. They are protected by private security. They despise students, forced into onerous debt peonage for their education, who are non-conformists, who defy their fiefdoms and call out their complicity in genocide.

Columbia University, with an endowment of $13.64 billion, charges students nearly $90,000 a year to attend. But students are not allowed to object when their tax and tuition money funds genocide, or when their tuition payments are used to see them, along with faculty supporters, assaulted and sent to jail. They are, as President Biden put it, members of "hate groups." They are—as Senate Majority leader Chuck Schumer said of those who occupied Hamilton Hall at Columbia, renaming it Hind Hall in honor of a five-year-old Palestinian girl, Hind Rajab, who was murdered by Israeli tank gunfire, after spending hours trapped in a car with her six dead relatives—engaged in "lawlessness."[172]

During the assault by dozens of police on the occupied hall, one student was knocked unconscious, several were beaten and sent to the hospital, and a shot was fired by a police officer inside the hall. The excess use of force is justified with the lie that there are outside infiltrators and agitators directing the protest.

"The university is a place of capital accumulation," says Sara Wexler, a doctoral student in philosophy, seated with two other students on the fire escape. "We have billion-dollar endowments that are connected to Israel and defense companies. We are being forced to confront the fact that universities aren't democratic. You have a board of trustees and investors that are actually making the decisions. Even if students have votes saying they want divestment and the faculty want divestment, we actually don't have any power because they can call in the NYPD."

There is an iron determination by the ruling institutions, including the media, to shift the narrative away from the genocide in Gaza to threats against Jewish students and anti-Semitism. The anger the protesters feel for journalists, especially at news organizations such as *CNN* and *The New York Times*, is intense and justified.

"I'm a German-Polish Jew," says Wexler. "My last name is Wexler. It's Yiddish for money-maker, money-exchanger. No matter how many times I tell people I'm Jewish, I'm still labeled anti-Semitic. It's infuriating. We are told that we need a state that is based on ethnicity in the twenty-first century and that's the only way Jewish people can be safe. But it is really for Britain and America and other imperialist states to have a presence in the Middle East. I've no idea why people still believe this narrative. It makes no sense to have a place for Jewish people that requires other people to suffer and die."

I have seen this assault on universities and freedom of expression before. I saw it in Augusto Pinochet's Chile, the military dictatorship in El Salvador, Guatemala under Rios Montt, and during my coverage of the military regimes in Argentina, Peru, Bolivia, Syria, Iraq, and Algeria.

Columbia University, with its locked gates, lines of police cruisers, rows of metal barricades three and four deep, swarms of uniformed police and private security, looks no different. It looks no different because it is no different.

The cacophony of the streets of New York City punctuates our conversation. These students know what they are risking. They know what they are up against.

Student activists waited months before setting up encampments. They tried repeatedly to have their voices heard and their concerns addressed. But they were rebuffed, ignored, and harassed. In November 2023, the students presented a petition to the university calling for divestment from Israeli corporations that facilitate the genocide. No one bothered to respond.

The protesters endure constant abuse. On April 25, during Columbia's senior boat cruise, Muslim students and those identified as supporting the protests, had alcohol poured on their heads and clothes by jeering Zionists. In January 2024, former Israeli soldiers studying at Columbia used skunk spray to assault students on the steps of Low Library.[173] The university, under heavy pressure once the attackers were identified, said they had banned the former soldiers from the university, but students reported seeing one of the men on campus. When Jewish students in the encampment attempted to prepare their meals in the kosher kitchen at the Jewish Theological Seminary, they were insulted by Zionists who were in the building. Zionist counter-demonstrators have been joined on campus by the founder of the white supremacist Proud Boys organization. Students have had their personal information posted on the Canary Mission and found their faces on the sides of trucks circling the campus, denouncing them as anti-Semites.[174]

These attacks are replicated at other universities, including the University of California, Los Angeles, where masked Zionists released mice and tossed fireworks into the encampment, and broadcasted the sound of crying children—something the Israeli army does to lure Palestinians in Gaza, out of hiding, to kill them.[175] The Zionist mob, armed with pepper and bear spray, violently attacked the protesters as police and campus security watched passively and refused to make arrests.

"At the General Studies gala, which is one of the undergraduate schools that has a large population of former IDF soldiers, at least eight students wearing keffiyehs were physically and verbally harassed by students identified as ex-IDF and Israelis," Cameron Jones, a sophomore majoring in urban studies and who is Jewish, tells me. "Students were called 'bitch' and 'whore' in Hebrew. Some were called terrorists and told to go back to Gaza. Many of the students harassed were Arabs, some having their keffiyehs ripped off and thrown to the ground. Several students in keffiyehs were grabbed and pushed. A Jewish student wearing a keffiyeh was cursed at in Hebrew and later punched in the face. Another student was kicked. The event ended after dozens of students sang the Israeli national anthem, some of them flipping off students wearing keffiyehs. I have been followed around campus by individuals and been cursed and had obscenities yelled at me."

The university has refused to reprimand those who disrupted the gala, even though the individuals who carried out the assaults have been identified.

Universities have hired people such as Cas Holloway, currently the chief operating officer at Columbia, who was the deputy mayor for operations under Michael Bloomberg. Holloway reportedly oversaw the police clearance of the Occupy encampment at Zuccotti Park. This is the kind of expertise universities covet.

Following the mass arrests and evictions from their encampment and Hind Hall, student organizers at Columbia called for university-wide strikes by faculty, staff, and students. Columbia canceled its university-wide commencement in the spring of 2024.

I am on the campus of Princeton University. It is after evening prayers and seventeen students who have mounted a hunger strike sit together, many wrapped in blankets.

As universities escalate their crackdowns, the protesters escalate their response. Students at Princeton held rallies and walk-outs throughout October and November 2023, which culminated in a protest at the Council of the Princeton University Community, made up of administrators, students, staff, deans, and the president. They were met at each protest with a wall of silence.

Princeton students decided, following the example at Columbia, to set up a tent encampment and issued a set of demands calling on the university to "divest and disassociate from Israel." But when they arrived early in the morning at their staging areas, as well as the site in front of Firestone Library, which they hoped to use for an encampment, they were met with dozens of campus police and Princeton town police who had been tipped off. The students hastily occupied another location on campus, McCosh Courtyard. Two students were immediately arrested, evicted from their student housing, and banned from campus. The police forced the remaining students to take down their tents.

Protesters at the encampment have been sleeping in the open, including when it rains.

In an irony not lost on the students, dotted around Princeton's campus are massive tents set up for reunion weekend where alumni down copious amounts of alcohol and dress up in garish outfits with the school colors of orange and black. The protesters are barred from entering them.

Thirteen students at Princeton occupied Clio Hall on April 29, 2024. They, like their counterparts at Columbia, were arrested and are now barred from campus. Some two hundred students surrounded Clio Hall in solidarity as the occupying students were led away by police. As they were being processed by the police, the arrested students sang the Black spiritual "Roll, Jordan, Roll," altering the words to "Well, some say John was a baptist, some say John was a Palestinian, but I say John was a preacher of God and my bible says so too."

The hunger strikers, who began their liquid-only diet on May 3, 2024, issued this statement:

> The Princeton Gaza Solidarity Encampment announces the initiation of a hunger strike in solidarity with the millions of Palestinians in Gaza suffering under the ongoing siege by the state of Israel. The Israeli occupation has deliberately blocked access to basic necessities to engineer a dire famine for the two million residents of Gaza. Since the announcement on October 9 by the Israeli Defense Minister prohibiting the entry of food, fuel and electricity into the Gaza Strip, Israel has systematically obstructed and limited access to vital aid for Palestinians in Gaza, even intentionally destroying existing cropland. On March 18, the UN Secretary General declared that "This is the highest number of people facing catastrophic hunger ever recorded by the integrated food security classification system." To make bread, Gazans have been forced to use animal feed as flour. To break their fasts in Ramadan, Gazans have been forced to prepare meals of grass. Ninety-seven percent of Gaza's water has been deemed undrinkable since October 2021 and they have been forced to drink dirty salt water to survive.
>
> The consequences of this unprecedented famine created and maintained by Israel will devastate Gaza's children for generations to come and cannot be tolerated any longer. We have begun our hunger strike to stand in solidarity with the people of Gaza. We are drawing from the tradition of Palestinian political prisoners going on salt-water-only hunger strikes in Israeli prisons since 1968.

Our hunger strike is a response to the administration's refusal to engage with our demands for disassociation and divestment from Israel. We refuse to be silenced by the university administration's intimidation and repression tactics. We struggle together in solidarity with the people of Palestine. We commit our bodies to their liberation. Participants in the hunger strikes will abstain from all food or drink except water until the following demands are met:

- Meet with students to discuss demands for disclosure, divestment and a full academic and cultural boycott of Israel.
- Grant complete amnesty from all criminal and disciplinary charges for participants of the peaceful sit-in.
- Reverse all campus bans and evictions of students.

University President Christopher Eisgruber met with the hunger strikers—the first meeting by school administrators with protesters since October 7—but dismissed their demands.

"This is probably the most important thing I've done here," says Areeq Hasan, a senior who is part of the hunger strike and who will begin a PhD in applied physics next year at Stanford. "If we're on a scale of one to ten, this is a ten. Since the start of encampment, I have tried to become a better person. We have pillars of faith. One of them is *sunnah*, which is prayer. That's a place where you train yourself to become a better person. It is linked to spirituality. That's something I've been emphasizing more during my time at Princeton. There's another aspect of faith. *Zakat*. It means charity, but you can read it more generally as justice . . . economic justice and social justice. I'm training myself, but to what end? This encampment is not just about trying to cultivate, to purify my heart to try to become a better person, but about trying to stand for justice and actively use these skills that I'm learning to command what I feel to be right and to forbid what I believe to be wrong, to stand up for oppressed people around the world."

Anha Khan, a Princeton student on hunger strike whose family is from Bangladesh, sits with her knees tucked up in front of her. She is wearing blue sweatpants that say Looney Tunes and an engagement ring that every so often glints in the light. She sees in Bangladesh's history of colonialism, dispossession, and genocide the experience of Palestinians.

"So much was taken from my people," she says. "We haven't had the time or the resources to recuperate from the terrible times we've gone through. Not only did my people go through a genocide in 1971, but we were also victims of the partition that happened in 1947 and then civil disputes between West and East Pakistan throughout the forties, the fifties, and the sixties. It makes me angry. If we weren't colonized by the British throughout the eighteenth, nineteenth, and twentieth century, and if we weren't occupied, we would have had time to develop and create a more prosperous society. Now we're staggering because so much was taken from us. It's not fair."

The hostility of the university has radicalized the students, who see university administrators attempting to placate external pressures from wealthy donors, the weapons manufacturers, and the Israel lobby, rather than deal with the internal realities of the nonviolent protests and the genocide.

"The administration doesn't care about the well-being, health, or safety of their students," Khan tells me. "We have tried to get at least tents out at night. Since we are on a twenty-four-hour liquid fast, not eating anything, our bodies are working overtime to stay resilient. Our immune systems are not as strong. Yet the university tells us we can't pitch up tents to keep ourselves safe at night from the cold and the winds. It's abhorrent for me. I feel a lot more physical weakness. My headaches are worse. There is an inability to even climb up stairs now. It made me realize that for the past seven months what Gazans have been facing is a million times worse. You can't understand their plight unless you experience that kind of starvation that they're experiencing, although I'm not experiencing the atrocities they're experiencing."

Though the hunger strikers receive support on social media, they have also been the targets of death threats and hateful messages from conservative influencers. "I give them ten hours before they call DoorDash," someone posted on X. "Why won't they give up water, don't they care about Palestine? Come on, give up water!" another post read. "Can they hold their breath too? Asking for a friend," another read. "OK so I hear there's going to be a bunch of barbecues at Princeton this weekend, let's bring out a bunch of pork products too to show these Muslims!" someone posted.

On campus the tiny groups of counter-protesters, many from the ultra-orthodox Chabad House, jeer at the protesters, shouting "Jihadists!" or "I like your terrorist headscarf!"

"It is horrifying to see thousands upon thousands of people wish for our deaths and hope that we starve and die," Khan says softly. "In the press release video, I wore a mask. One of the funnier comments I got was, 'Wow, I bet that chick on the right has buck-teeth behind that mask.' It's ridiculous. Another read, 'I bet that chick on the right used her Dyson Supersonic before coming to the press release.' The Dyson Supersonic is a really expensive hair dryer. Honestly, the only thing I got from that was that my hair looked good, so thank you!"

David Chmielewski, a senior whose parents are Polish and who had family interned in the Nazi death camps, is a Muslim convert. His visits to the concentration camps in Poland, including Auschwitz, made him acutely aware of the capacity for human evil. He sees this evil in the genocide in Gaza. He sees the same indifference and support that characterized Nazi Germany. "Never again," he says, "means never again for everyone."

"Since the genocide, the university has failed to reach out to Arab students, to Muslim students and to Palestinian students to offer support," he tells me. "The university claims it is committed to diversity, equity and inclusion, but we don't feel we belong here.

"We're told in our Islamic tradition by our prophets that when one part of the *ummah*, the nation of believers, feels pain, then we all feel pain," he says. "That has to be an important motivation for us. But the second part is that Islam gives us an obligation to strive for justice regardless of who we're striving on behalf of. There are plenty of Palestinians who aren't Muslim, but we're fighting for the liberation of all Palestinians. Muslims stand up for issues that aren't specifically Muslim issues. There were Muslims who were involved in the struggle against apartheid in South Africa. There were Muslims involved in the Civil Rights Movement. We draw inspiration from them.

"This is a beautiful interfaith struggle," he says. "Yesterday, we set up a tarp where we were praying. We had people doing group Quran recitations. On the same tarp, Jewish students had their Shabbat service. On Sunday, we had Christian services at the encampment. We are trying to give a vision of the world that we want to build, a world after apartheid. We're not just responding to Israeli apartheid, we're trying to build our own vision of what a society would look like. That's what you see when you have people doing Quran recitations or reading Shabbat services on the same tarp, that's the kind of world we want to build."

"We've been portrayed as causing people to feel unsafe," he says. "We've been perceived as presenting a threat. Part of the motivation for the hunger strike is making clear that we're not the people making anyone unsafe. The university is making us unsafe. They're unwilling to meet with us and we're willing to starve ourselves. Who's causing the un-safety? There is a hypocrisy about how we're being portrayed. We're being portrayed as violent when it's the universities who are calling police on peaceful protesters. We're being portrayed as disrupting everything around us, but what we're drawing on are traditions fundamental to American political culture. We're drawing on traditions of sit-ins, hunger strikes, and peaceful encampments. Palestinian political prisoners have carried out hunger strikes for decades. The hunger strike goes back to decolonial struggles before that, to India, to Ireland, to the struggle against apartheid in South Africa.

"Palestinian liberation is the cause of human liberation," he goes on. "Palestine is the most obvious example in the world today, other than the United States, of settler colonialism. The struggle against Zionist occupation is viewed accurately by Zionists, both within the United States and Israel, as sort of the last dying gasp of imperialism. They're trying to hold onto it. That's why it's scary. The liberation of Palestine would mean a radically different world, a world that moves past exploitation and injustice. That's why so many people who aren't Palestinian and aren't Arab and aren't Muslim are so invested in this struggle. They see its significance."

"In quantum mechanics there's the idea of non-locality," says Hasan. "Even though I'm miles and miles away from the people in Palestine, I feel deeply entangled with them in the same way that the electrons that I work with in my lab are entangled. As David said, this idea that the community of believers is one body and if one part of the body is in pain, all of it pains; it is our responsibility to strive to alleviate that pain. If we take a step back and look at this composite system, it's evolving in perfect unitary, even though we don't understand it because we only have access to one small piece of it. There is deep underlying justice that maybe we don't recognize, but that exists when we look at the plight of the Palestinian people."

"There's a tradition associated with the prophet," he says. "When you've seen an injustice occur you should try to change it with your hands. If you can't change it with your hands, then you should try to adjust it with your tongue. You should speak out about it. If you can't do that, you should at least feel the injustice in your heart. This hunger strike, this encampment, everything we're doing here as students is my way of trying to realize that, trying to implement that in my life."

Spend time with the students in the protests and you hear stories of revelations, epiphanies. In the lexicon of Christianity, these are called moments of grace. These experiences, these moments of grace, are the unseen engine of the protest movements.

When Oscar Lloyd, a junior at Columbia studying cognitive science and philosophy, was about eight years old, he and his family visited the Pine Ridge Reservation in South Dakota.

"I saw the vast distinction between the huge memorial at the Battle of the Little Bighorn compared to the small wooden sign at the massacre at Wounded Knee," he says, comparing the numerous monuments celebrating the 1876 defeat of the US Seventh Cavalry at the Little Bighorn to the massacre of two hundred and fifty to three hundred Native Americans, half of whom were women and children, in 1890 at Wounded Knee. "I was shocked that there can be two sides to history, that one side can be told and the other can be completely forgotten. This is the story of Palestine."

Sara Ryave, a graduate student at Princeton, spent a year in Israel studying at the Pardes Institute of Jewish Studies, a non-denominational yeshiva. She came face to face with apartheid. She was banned from campus after occupying Clio Hall.

"It was during that year that I saw things that I will never forget," she said. "I spent time in the West Bank and with communities in the South Hebron Hills. I saw the daily realities of apartheid. If you don't look for them, you don't notice them. But once you do, if you want to, it's clear. That predisposed me to this. I saw people living under police and IDF military threats every single day, whose lives are made unbearable by settlers."

When Hasan was in fourth grade, he remembers his mother weeping uncontrollably on the twenty-seventh night during Ramadan, an especially holy time known as The Night of Power. On this night, prayers are traditionally answered.

"I have a very vivid memory of standing in prayer at night next to my mother," he says. "My mother was weeping. I'd never seen her cry so much in my life. I remember that so vividly. I asked her why she was crying. She told me that she was crying because of all of the people that were suffering around the world. And among them, I can imagine she was bringing to heart the people in Palestine. At that point in my life, I didn't understand systems of oppression. But what I did understand was that I'd never seen my mother in such pain before. I didn't want her to be in that kind of pain. My sister and I, seeing our mother in so much pain, started crying too. The emotions were so strong that night. I don't think I've ever cried like that in my life. That was the first time I had a consciousness of suffering in the world, specifically systems of oppression, though I didn't really understand the various dimensions of it until much later on. That's when my heart established a connection to the plight of the Palestinian people."

Hellen Wainaina, a doctoral student in English who occupied Clio Hall at Princeton and who is barred from campus, was born in South Africa. She lived in Tanzania until she was ten years old and then moved with her family to Houston.

"I think of my parents and their journeys in Africa and eventually leaving the African continent," she says. "I'm conflicted that they ended up in the US. If things had turned out differently during the postcolonial movements, they would not have moved. We would have been able to live, grow up, and study where we were. I've always felt that that was a profound injustice. I'm grateful that my parents did everything they could to get us here, but I remember when I got my citizenship, I was very angry. I had no say. I wish the world was oriented differently, that we didn't need to come here, that the postcolonial dreams of people who worked on those movements actually materialized."

The protest movements—which have spread around the globe—are not built around the single issue of the apartheid state in Israel or its genocide against Palestinians. They are built around the awareness that the old world order, the one of settler colonialism, Western imperialism, and militarism, used by the countries in the Global North to dominate the Global South, must end. They decry the hoarding of natural resources and wealth by industrial nations in a world of diminishing returns. These protests are built around a vision of a world of equality, dignity, and independence. This vision, and the commitment to it, will make this movement not only hard to defeat, but presages a wider struggle beyond the genocide in Gaza.

The genocide has awakened a sleeping giant. Let us pray the giant prevails.

Achinthya Sivalingam, a graduate student in Public Affairs at Princeton University, did not know when she woke up early on the morning of April 25, 2024 that shortly after 7 a.m. she would join hundreds of students across the country who have been arrested, evicted, and banned from campus for protesting the genocide in Gaza.

She wears a blue sweatshirt, sometimes fighting back tears, when I speak to her. We are seated at a table in the Small World Coffee shop on Witherspoon Street, half a block away from the university she can no longer enter, from the apartment she can no longer live in, and from the campus where in a few weeks she was scheduled to graduate.

She wonders where she will spend the night.

The police gave her five minutes to collect items from her apartment.

"I grabbed really random things," she says. "I grabbed oatmeal for whatever reason. I was really confused."

Student protesters across the country exhibit a moral and physical courage—many are facing suspension and expulsion—that shames every major institution in the country. They are dangerous not because they disrupt campus life or engage in attacks on Jewish students—many of those protesting are Jewish—but because they expose the abject failure of the ruling elites and their institutions to halt genocide, the crime of crimes. These students watch, like most of us, Israel's live-streamed slaughter of the Palestinian people. But unlike most of us, they act. Their voices and protests are a potent counterpoint to the moral bankruptcy that surrounds them.

Not one university president has denounced Israel's destruction of every university in Gaza. Not one university president has called for an immediate and unconditional ceasefire. Not one university president has used the words "apartheid" or "genocide." Not one university president has called for sanctions and divestment from Israel.

Instead, heads of these academic institutions grovel supinely before wealthy donors, corporations—including weapons manufacturers—and rabid right-wing politicians. They reframe the debate around harm to Jews rather than the daily slaughter of Palestinians, including thousands of children. They have allowed the abusers—the Zionist state and its supporters—to paint themselves as victims. This false narrative, which focuses on anti-Semitism, allows the centers of power, including the media, to block out the real issues—land theft and genocide. It contaminates the debate. It is a classic case of "reactive abuse." Raise your voice to decry injustice, react to prolonged abuse, attempt to resist, and the abuser suddenly transforms themself into the aggrieved.

Over the summer of 2024, universities and colleges across the country hired "risk and crisis management" consulting firms, many with ties to Israel, to formulate policies to criminalize the most tepid forms of dissent. They imposed bans on encampments, temporary structures, amplified sound, chalking, freestanding signs, flyering, outdoor displays, and events tables. A whisper of protest inside or outside a classroom will see faculty and students censored, suspended, or expelled.

The university administration at Princeton knew about the proposed encampment in advance. When the students reached the five staging sites on April 25, 2024, they were met by large numbers from the university's Department of Public Safety and the Princeton Police Department. The site of the proposed encampment in front of Firestone Library was filled with police. This is despite the fact that students kept their plans off university emails and confined to what they thought were secure apps. Standing among the police this morning was Rabbi Eitan Webb, who founded and heads Princeton's Chabad House. He has attended university events to vocally attack those who advocate for an end to the genocide, according to student activists. Rabbi Webb would later visit the encampment to taunt protestors and accuse them of being anti-Semites.

As I stand with some hundred protesters listening to speakers, a helicopter circles noisily overhead. A banner hanging from a tree reads: "From the River to the Sea, Palestine Will be Free."

The students say they will continue their protest until Princeton divests from firms that "profit from or engage in the State of Israel's ongoing military campaign" in Gaza; ends university research "on weapons of war" funded by the Department of Defense; enacts an academic and cultural boycott of Israeli institutions; supports Palestinian academic and cultural institutions; and advocates for an immediate and unconditional ceasefire.

However, if the students again attempt to erect tents—they took down fourteen tents once the two arrests were made—it seems certain they will all be arrested.

"It is far beyond what I expected to happen," says Aditi Rao, a doctoral student in classics. "They started arresting people seven minutes into the encampment."

Princeton Vice President of Campus Life Rochelle Calhoun sent out a mass email warning students they could be arrested and thrown off campus if they erected an encampment.

"Any individual involved in an encampment, occupation, or other unlawful disruptive conduct who refuses to stop after a warning will be arrested and immediately barred from campus," she wrote. "For students, such exclusion from campus would jeopardize their ability to complete the semester."

These students, she added, could be suspended or expelled.

Sivalingam ran into one of her professors and pleaded with him for faculty support for the protest. He informed her he was coming up for tenure and could not participate. The course he teaches is called "Ecological Marxism."

"It was a bizarre moment," she says. "I spent last semester thinking about ideas and evolution and civil change, like social change. It was a crazy moment."

She starts to cry.

A few minutes after 7 a.m., police distributed a leaflet to the students erecting tents with the headline "Princeton University Warning and No Trespass Notice." The leaflet stated that the students were "engaged in conduct on Princeton University property that violates University rules and regulations, poses a threat to the safety and property of others, and disrupts the regular operations of the University: such conduct includes participating in an encampment and/or disrupting a University event." The leaflet said those who engaged in the "prohibited conduct" would be considered a "Defiant Trespasser under New Jersey criminal law (N.J.S.A. 2C:18-3) and subject to immediate arrest."

A few seconds later Sivalingam heard a police officer say, "Get those two."

Hassan Sayed, a doctoral student in economics who is of Pakistani descent, was working with Sivalingam to erect one of the tents. He was handcuffed. Sivalingam was zip-tied so tightly it cut off circulation to her hands. There are dark bruises circling her wrists.

"There was an initial warning from cops about 'You are trespassing' or something like that, 'This is your first warning,'" Sayed says. "It was kind of loud. I didn't hear too much. Suddenly, hands were thrust behind my back. As this happened, my right arm tensed a bit and they said 'You are resisting arrest if you do that.' They put the handcuffs on."

He was asked by one of the arresting officers if he was a student. When he said he was, they immediately informed him that he was banned from campus.

"No mention of what charges are as far as I could hear," he says. "I get taken to one car. They pat me down a bit. They ask for my student ID."

Sayed was placed in the back of a campus police car with Sivalingam, who was in agony from the zip ties. He asked the police to loosen the zip ties on Sivalingam, a process that took several minutes as they had to remove her from the vehicle, and the scissors were unable to cut through the plastic. They had to find wire cutters. They were taken to the university's police station.

Sayed was stripped of his phone, keys, clothes, backpack, and AirPods and placed in a holding cell. No one read him his Miranda rights.

He was again told he was banned from the campus.

"Is this an eviction?" he asked the campus police.

The police did not answer.

He asked to call a lawyer. He was told he could call a lawyer when the police were ready.

"They may have mentioned something about trespassing, but I don't remember clearly," he says. "It certainly was not made salient to me."

He was told to fill out forms about his mental health and if he was on medication. Then he was informed he was being charged with "defiant trespassing."

"I say, 'I'm a student, how is that trespassing? I attend school here,'" he says. "They really don't seem to have a good answer. I reiterate, asking whether me being banned from campus constitutes eviction because I live on campus. They just say, 'ban from campus.' I said something like that doesn't answer the question. They say it will all be explained in the letter. I'm like, 'Who is writing the letter?' 'Dean of grad school,' they respond."

Sayed was driven to his campus housing. The campus police

did not let him have his keys. He was given a few minutes to grab items like his phone charger. They locked his apartment door. He, too, is seeking shelter in the Small World Coffee shop.

Sivalingam often returned to Tamil Nadu in southern India, where she was born, for her summer vacations. She says the poverty and daily struggle of those around her to survive were "sobering."

"The disparity of my life and theirs, how to reconcile how those things exist in the same world," she says, her voice quivering with emotion. "It was always very bizarre to me. I think that's where a lot of my interest in addressing inequality, in being able to think about people outside of the United States as humans, as people who deserve lives and dignity, comes from."

She must adjust to being exiled from campus.

"I gotta find somewhere to sleep," she says, "tell my parents, but that's going to be a little bit of a conversation, and find ways to engage in jail support and communications because I can't be there, but I can continue to mobilize."

There are many shameful periods in American history. "Indian Removal" and the genocide we carried out against Indigenous peoples. Slavery. The violent suppression of the labor movement that saw hundreds of workers killed. Lynching. Jim and Jane Crow. Vietnam. Iraq. Afghanistan. Libya.

The genocide in Gaza, which we fund and support, is of such monstrous proportions that it will achieve a prominent place in this pantheon of crimes.

History will not be kind to most of us. But it will bless and revere these students.

# XI

# LETTER TO THE CHILDREN OF GAZA

Dear child. It is past midnight. I am flying at hundreds of miles an hour in the darkness, thousands of feet over the Atlantic Ocean. I am traveling to Egypt. I will go to the border of Gaza at Rafah. I go because of you.

You have never been in a plane. You have never left Gaza. You know only the densely packed streets and alleys. The concrete hovels. You know only the security barriers and fences patrolled by soldiers that surround Gaza. Planes, for you, are terrifying. Fighter jets. Attack helicopters. Drones. They circle above you. They drop missiles and bombs. Deafening explosions. The ground shakes. Buildings fall. The dead. The screams. The muffled calls for help from beneath the rubble. It does not stop. Night and day. Trapped under the piles of smashed concrete. Your playmates. Your schoolmates. Your neighbors. Gone in seconds. You see the chalky faces and limp bodies when they are dug out.

I am a reporter. It is my job to see this. You are a child. You should never see this.

The stench of death. Rotting corpses under broken concrete. You hold your breath. You cover your mouth with cloth. You walk faster. Your neighborhood has become a graveyard. All that was familiar is gone. You stare in amazement. You wonder where you are.

You are afraid. Explosion after explosion. You cry. You cling to your mother or father. You cover your ears. You see the white light of the missile and wait for the blast. Why do they kill children? What did you do? Why can't anyone protect you? Will you be wounded? Will you lose a leg or an arm? Will you go blind or be in a wheelchair? Why were you born? Was it for something good? Or was it for this? Will you grow up? Will you be happy? What will it be like without your friends? Who will die next? Your mother? Your father? Your brothers and sisters? Someone you know will be injured. Soon. Someone you know will die. Soon.

At night you lie in the dark on the cold cement floor. The phones are cut. The internet is off. You do not know what is happening. There are flashes of light. There are waves of blast concussions. There are screams. It does not stop.

When your father or mother hunts for food or water, you wait. That terrible feeling in your stomach. Will they come back? Will you see them again? Will your tiny home be next? Will the bombs find you? Are these your last moments on earth?

You drink salty, dirty water. It makes you very sick. Your stomach hurts. You are hungry. The bakeries are destroyed. There is no bread. You eat one meal a day. Pasta. A cucumber. Soon this will seem like a feast.

You do not play with your soccer ball made of rags. You do not fly your kite made from old newspapers.

You have seen foreign reporters. We wear flak jackets with the word PRESS written on them. We have helmets. We have cameras. We drive Jeeps. We appear after a bombing or a shooting. We sit over coffee for a long time and talk to the adults. Then we disappear. We do not usually interview children. But I have done interviews when groups of you crowded around us. Laughing. Pointing. Asking us to take your picture.

I have been bombed by jets in Gaza. I have been bombed in other wars, wars that happened before you were born. I too was very, very scared. I still have dreams about it. When I see the pictures of Gaza, these wars return to me with the force of thunder and lightning. I think of you.

All of us who have been to war hate war most of all because of what it does to children.

I tried to tell your story. I tried to tell the world that when you are cruel to people, week after week, month after month, year after year, decade after decade, when you deny people freedom and dignity, when you humiliate and trap them in an open-air prison, when you kill them as if they were beasts, they become very angry. They do to others what was done to them. I told it over and over. I told it for seven years. Few listened. And now this.

There are very brave Palestinian journalists. More than one hundred of them have been killed since this bombing began. They are heroes. So are the doctors and nurses in your hospitals. So are the UN workers, over two hundred of whom have died.[176] So are the ambulance drivers and the medics. So are the rescue parties that lift up the slabs of concrete with their hands. So are the mothers and fathers who shield you from the bombs.

But we are not there. Not this time. We cannot get in. We are locked out.

Reporters from all over the world are going to the border crossing at Rafah. We are going because we cannot watch this slaughter and do nothing. We are going because hundreds of people are dying every day, including many children. We are going because this genocide must stop. We are going because we have children. Like you. Precious. Innocent. Loved. We are going because we want you to live.

I hope one day we will meet. You will be an adult. I will be an old man, although to you, I am already very old. In my dream for you I will find you free and safe and happy. No one will be trying to kill you. You will fly in airplanes filled with people, not bombs. You will not be trapped in a concentration camp. You will see the world. You will grow up and have children. You will become old.

You will remember this suffering, but you will know it means you must help others who suffer.

This is my hope. My prayer.

We have failed you. This is the awful guilt we carry. We tried. But we did not try hard enough. We will go to Rafah. Many of us. Reporters. We will stand outside the border with Gaza in protest. We will write and film. This is what we do. It is not much. But it is something. We will tell your story again.

Maybe it will be enough to earn the right to ask for your forgiveness.

# ACKNOWLEDGMENTS

For over a year, the focus of my writing and my show, *The Chris Hedges Report,* has been on the genocide in Gaza. The material in this book is primarily taken from the columns and shows that seek to shine a light on the struggle of the Palestinians and their decades-long conflict with the apartheid state of Israel.

I owe a huge debt to Naila Kauser and Mohamed Elmaazi, as well as Narda Zacchino, Christopher Renshaw, and Sofia Menemenlis, who did the copyediting and fact-checking. Robert Scheer, the editor-in-chief of *ScheerPost,* broadened and focused much of the writing. Dan Simon, the publisher of Seven Stories Press, and Greg Ruggiero conceived of this project. I am grateful for their help. Dwayne Booth, aka Mr. Fish, provides the searing and brilliant illustrations for my columns. I would not be able to produce *The Chris Hedges Report* without Max Jones, Diego Ramos, Thomas Hedges, and Sofia Menemenlis. They created *The Chris Hedges Report* after my show on *The Real News Network* was terminated, and bring to it an exacting professionalism.

I have made three trips to the Middle East since October 7, 2023, spending weeks in Egypt, where I have been twice, Jordan, the occupied West Bank, and Qatar, where I appeared on *Al Jazeera English* and *Al Jazeera Arabic.* I would be remiss without thanking my wonderful Arabic teachers Omar Othman, Rafah Al-Siyoufi, Sary Awad, and Ruba Jaffer. They are not only my teachers, but cherished friends. Finally, I want to thank Eunice, who is, along with all her many other talents, a skilled editor. She is the final authority on everything I write.

You can find my writing and my shows at chrishedges.substack.com.

# BIBLIOGRAPHY

Abu Saif, Atef. *Don't Look Left: A Diary of Genocide*. Boston: Beacon Press, 2024.

Arendt, Hannah. *The Origins of Totalitarianism*. New York: Harcourt Brace, 1976.

Auden, W.H. *Selected Poems*. Edited by Edward Mendelson. London: Faber and Faber, 1979.

Baroud, Ramzy. *My Father Was a Freedom Fighter: Gaza's Untold Story*. London: Pluto Press, 2010.

Barsamian, David. *The Pen and the Sword: Conversations with Edward Said*. Monroe: Common Courage Press, 1994.

Benjamin, Walter. "Critique of Violence," in *Reflections: Essays, Aphorisms, and Autobiographical Writings*. Trans. Edmund Jephcott, Ed. Peter Demetz. New York: Schocken Books, 1978.'

Benjamin, Walter. "Goethe's Elective Affinities," in *Selected Writings, Volume 1, 1913-1926*. Ed. Marcus Bullock and Michael W. Jennings. Cambridge, MA and London: Belknap Press, 1996.

Berrigan, Daniel. *The Trial of the Catonsville Nine*. Boston: Beacon Press, 1970.

Blumenthal, Max. *Goliath: Life and Loathing in Greater Israel*. New York: Nation Books, 2013.

Blumenthal, Max. *The 51 Day War: Ruin and Resistance in Gaza*. New York: Nation Books, 2015.

Bowker, Robert. *Palestinian Refugees: Mythology, Identity, and the Search for Peace*. Boulder: Lynne Rienner Publishers, 2003.

Borowski, Tadeusz. *This Way for the Gas, Ladies and Gentlemen*. New York: Penguin Classics, 1976.

Browning, Christopher R. *Ordinary Men: Reserve Police Battalion 101 and the Final Solution in Poland*. New York: HarperPerennial, 1992.

Chomsky, Noam. *Fateful Triangle: The United States, Israel & The Palestinians*. London: Pluto Press, 1999.

Chomsky, Noam and Ilan Pappé. *Gaza in Crisis: Reflections on Israel's War against the Palestinians*. Edited by Frank Barat. London: Haymarket Books, 2010.

Darwish, Mahmoud. Translated by Fady Joudah. *The Butterfly's Burden*. Port Townsend: Copper Canyon Press, 2007.

Duras, Marguerite. *The War: A Memoir*. New York: Pantheon, 1986.

Edelman, Marek. *The Ghetto Fights*. Chicago: Bookmarks, 1990.

Farsoun, Samih K., with Christina E. Zacharia. *Palestine and the Palestinians*. Boulder: Westview Press, 1997.

Finkelstein, Norman G. *Gaza: An Inquest Into Its Martyrdom*. Oakland: University of California Press, 2018.

Finkelstein, Norman G. *The Holocaust Industry: Reflections on the Exploitation of Jewish Suffering*. New York: Verso Books, 2000.

Fisk, Robert. *The Great War for Civilization: The Conquest of the Middle East*. New York: Alfred A. Knopf, 2006.

Fisk, Robert. *Pity the Nation: The Abduction of Lebanon*. New York: Antheum, 1990.

Fisk, Robert. *The Age of the Warrior*. New York: Nation Books, 2008.

Fromkin, David. *A Peace to End All Peace: Creating the Modern Middle East 1914-1922*. London: Andre Deutsch,1989.

Gordon, Neve. *Israel's Occupation*. Berkeley: University of California Press, 2008.

Gray, J. Glenn. *The Warriors: Reflections on Men in Battle*. Lincoln: University of Nebraska Press, 1998.

Halper, Jeff. *War Against the People*. London: Pluto Press, 2015.

Hass, Amira. *Drinking the Sea at Gaza: Days and Nights in a Land Under Siege*. London: Picador, 2000.

Hedges, Chris. *War is a Force That Gives Us Meaning*. New York: Public Affairs, 2014.

Heschel, Abraham Joshua. *The Prophets*. New York: Harper & Row, 1969.

Hilberg, Raul. *The Destruction of the European Jews, Vol. I, II, III*. New Haven: Yale University Press, 2003.

Kamel, Lorenzo. *Imperial Perceptions of Palestine: British Influence and Power in Late Ottoman Times*, (I.B. Tauris: Croydon, 2015)

Khalidi, Rashid. *The Hundred Years' War on Palestine: A History of Settler Colonialism and Resistance, 1917-2017*. New York: Metropolitan Books, 2020.

Khouri, Mounah A., and Hamid Algar, eds. and trans. *An Anthology of Modern Arabic Poetry*. Berkeley: University of California Press, 1974.

Le Bon, Gustave. *The Crowd: A Study of the Popular Mind*. Mineola, NY: Dover Publications, 2002.

Levi, Primo. *The Drowned and the Saved* translated by Raymond Rosenthal, (London: Michael Joseph, Penguin Group, 1988).

Levi, Primo. "The Gray Zone," In *The Holocaust: Origins, Implementation, Aftermath*, ed. Omer Bartov, 251-272, (Routledge: 2001)

Levi, Primo. *Moments of Reprieve*. Translated by Ruth Feldman. New York: Penguin, 1987.

Levy, Gideon. *The Punishment of Gaza*. New York: Verso Books, 2010.

Levy, Gideon. *The Killing Of Gaza: Reports on a Catastrophe*. New York: Verso Books, 2024.

Lindqvist, Sven. Translated by Joan Tate. *Exterminate All the Brutes: One Man's Odyssey into the Heart of Darkness and the Origins of European Genocide*. New York: The New Press, 1992.

Loewenstein, Antony. *The Palestine Laboratory: How Israel Exports the Technology of Occupation Around the World.* London: Verso Books, 2023.

Morris, Benny. *Righteous Victims: A History of the Zionist-Arab Conflict, 1881-2001.* New York: Vintage Books, 1999.

Niebuhr, Reinhold. *Moral Man and Immoral Society.* New York: Charles Scribner's Sons, 1960.

Niebuhr, Reinhold. "The Twilight of Liberalism," *New Republic,* June 14, 1919.

Nhất Hạnh, Thích. *Vietnam: Lotus in a Sea of Fire.* New York: Hill and Wang, 1967.

Pappé, Ilan. *The Ethnic Cleansing of Palestine.* Oxford: OneWorld Publications, 2006.

Pappé, Ilan. *The Biggest Prison on Earth: A History of the Occupied Territories.* London: OneWorld  Publications, 2019.

Pappé, Ilan. *Lobbying for Zionism.* London: OneWorld Publications, 2024.

Rogan, Eugene. *The Fall of the Ottomans.* New York: Basic Books, 2015.

Sacco, Joe. *Palestine.* Seattle: Fanagraphics Books, 2015.

Sacco, Joe. *Footnotes in Gaza.* New York: Metropolitan Books, 2009

Said, Edward W. *The End of the Peace Process: Oslo and After.* New York: Vintage Books, 2000.

Said, Edward W. *The Question of Palestine.* New York: Vintage Books, 1992.

Sand, Shlomo. *The Invention of the Jewish People.* Brooklyn: Verso Books, 2009.

Shlaim, Avi. *The Iron Wall: Israel and the Arab World.* New York: Penguin Books, 2000.

Shlaim, Avi. *Three Worlds: Memoirs of an Arab-Jew.* London: Oneworld Publications, 2024.

Stern-Weiner, Jamie, (Editor). *Deluge: Gaza and Israel From Crisis to Cataclysm.* New York: OR Books, 2024.

Tacitus. *Annals.* Translated by Cynthia Damon. London: Penguin Classics, 2012.

Toller, Ernst. *I Was a German: The Autobiography of a Revolutionary.* New York: Paragon House,1991.

Yergin, Daniel. *The Prize: The Epic Quest for Oil, Money & Power.* New York: Simon & Schuster, 1991.

# NOTES

1.  Mahmoud Darwish (محمود درویش), *Pride and Fury, in An Anthology of Modern Arabic Poetry*, ed. and trans. Mounah A. Khouri and Hamid Algar, (Berkeley and Los Angeles, CA, and London: University of California Press, 1974), 229-231.
2.  Amnesty International, "The Occupation of Water," November 29, 2017, *Amnesty International website,* accessed July 31, 2024, https://www.amnesty.org/en/latest/campaigns/2019/01/chapter--israeli-settlements-and-international-law/.
3.  Kevin Whelan and Andy Pollack, "Interview with Edward W. Said," *Postcolonial Text*, Vol 3, No 3 (2007), accessed July 31, 2024, https://www.postcolonial.org/index.php/pct/article/view/790/474.
4.  Francesca Albanese, "Genocide as colonial erasure," Report of the Special Rapporteur on the situation of human rights in the Palestinian territory occupied since 1967, United Nations General Assembly, October 1, 2024, accessed October 28, 2024, https://documents.un.org/doc/undoc/gen/n24/279/68/pdf/n2427968.pdf?utm_source=substack&utm_medium=email
5.  International Federation of Journalists, "Palestine: At Least 128 Journalists and Media Workers Killed in Gaza," IFJ, accessed September 30, 2024, archived via https://web.archive.org/web/20241007170732/https://www.ifj.org/media-centre/news/detail/category/press-releases/article/palestine-at-least-129-journalists-and-media-workers-killed-in-gaza.
6.  Euro-Med Human Rights Monitor, "Israeli Strike on Refaat al-Areer Apparently Deliberate," December 8, 2023, accessed August 4, 2024), *Euro-Med Monitor*, https://euromedmonitor.org/en/article/6014/Israeli-Strike-on-Refaat-al-Areer-Apparently-Deliberate.
7.  "If I Must Die,' a Poem by Refaat Alareer," *In These Times*, December 27, 2023, accessed August 4, 2024, https://inthesetimes.com/article/refaat-alareer-israeli-occupation-palestine.
8.  Atef Abu Saif, "I'm still alive. Gaza is no longer Gaza," *The Washington Post*, October 30, 2023, https://www.washingtonpost.com/opinions/2023/10/30/gaza-diary-war-explosions-death-hospital-fear/.
9.  Ibid.
10. Ibid.
11. Atef Abu Saif, *Don't Look Left: A Diary of Genocide*, (Boston: Beacon Press, 2024), 8.
12. Atef Abu Saif, "I'm still alive. Gaza is no longer Gaza," *The Washington Post*, October 30, 2023, https://www.washingtonpost.com/opinions/2023/10/30/gaza-diary-war-explosions-death-hospital-fear/.
13. Ibid.
14. Ibid.
15. Doctors, aid workers and UN officials have for months reported that operations—including cesarean sections on pregnant women and amputations of adults and children—have had to be performed without aesthetic and other crucial medical supplies, since Oct. 7 2023. See Bel Trew, "Inside Gaza's destroyed healthcare system: 'Children scream in pain as we operate without painkillers'," *The Independent*, July 10, 2024, accessed August 1, 2024, https://www.independent.co.uk/news/world/middle-east/gaza-war-israel-hospital-doctor-b2576536.html and United Nations Children's Fund,

et al, "Joint statement by UNICEF, WHO, UNFPA and UNRWA on Women and newborns bearing the brunt of the conflict in Gaza," *UNICEF website*, November 3, 2023, accessed August 1, 2024, https://www.unicef.org/press-releases/joint-statement-unicef-who-unfpa-and-unrwa-women-and-newborns-bearing-brunt-conflict.

16.    Atef Abu Saif, "I'm still alive. Gaza is no longer Gaza," *The Washington Post*, October 30, 2023, https://www.washingtonpost.com/opinions/2023/10/30/gaza-diary-war-explosions-death-hospital-fear/.

17.    Atef Abu Saif, "'The Horror That's Become Normal in Gaza," *Slate*, November 30, 2023, accessed August 4, 2024, https://slate.com/news-and-politics/2023/11/israel-gaza-war-diary-palestinian-experience-jabalia.html.

18.    Atef Abu Saif, *Don't Look Left: A Diary of Genocide*, (Boston: Beacon Press, 2024), 163.

19.    Atef Abu Saif, "I'm still alive. Gaza is no longer Gaza," *The Washington Post*, October 30, 2023, https://www.washingtonpost.com/opinions/2023/10/30/gaza-diary-war-explosions-death-hospital-fear/.

20.    The Associated Press, "Palestinian Man Killed After Israeli Settlers Storm Village in West Bank," *NBC News*, April 13, 2024, accessed August 4, 2024, https://www.nbcnews.com/news/world/palestinian-killed-israeli-settlers-storm-village-troops-fire-stone-th-rcna147688.

21.    Al Jazeera, "Israel's Smotrich Promises 'A Million' New Settlers Under Expansion Plan," June 28, 2024, *Al Jazeera*, accessed August 4, 2024, https://www.aljazeera.com/program/newsfeed/2024/6/28/israels-smotrich-promises-a-million-new-settlers-under-expansion-plan.

22.    Atef Abu Saif, *Don't Look Left: A Diary of Genocide*, (Boston: Beacon Press, 2024), 68.

23.    Joe Sacco, *Footnotes in Gaza*, (New York: Metropolitan Books, 2009), ix.

24.    Ali Abunimah, "Israeli Army Chief Praises PA Collaborators in Occupied West Bank," *The Electronic Intifada*, November 2, 2023, accessed September 30, 2024, https://electronicintifada.net/blogs/ali-abunimah/israeli-army-chief-praises-pa-collaborators-occupied-west-bank.

25.    W. H. Auden, *Selected Poems*, ed. Edward Mendelson, (London: Faber and Faber, 1979), 86.

26.    United States Holocaust Memorial Museum, "Chaim Engel describes his role in the Sobibor uprising," *Holocaust Encyclopedia*, accessed August 4, 2024, https://encyclopedia.ushmm.org/content/en/oral-history/chaim-engel-describes-his-role-in-the-sobibor-uprising.

27.    J. Glenn Gray, *The Warriors: Reflections On Men In Battle*, 2nd ed., (Lincoln: University of Nebraska Press, 1998), 139.

28.    Ibid., 169.

29.    Marguerite Duras, 1st ed. *The War: A Memoir*, (New York: Pantheon Books, 1986), 129 – 136.

30.    Asa Winstanley, "Israel killed Israelis, confirms new 7 October documentary," *The Electronic Intifada*, March 11, 2024, accessed August 4, 2024, https://electronicintifada.net/blogs/asa-winstanley/israel-killed-israelis-confirms-new-7-october-documentary. See also, Yaniv Kubovich, "IDF Ordered Hannibal Directive on October 7 to Prevent Hamas Taking Soldiers Captive," *Haaretz*, Jul 7, 2024, accessed August 4, 2024, https://www.haaretz.com/israel-news/2024-07-07/ty-article-magazine/.premium/idf-ordered-hannibal-directive-on-october-7-to-prevent-hamas-taking-soldiers-captive/00000190-89a2-d776-a3b1-fdbe45520000

31.    Nir Hasson, "In the Surrounding Kibbutzim They Try to Look Ahead" [in Hebrew], *Haaretz*, October 20, 2023, accessed August 4, 2024 https://www.haaretz.co.il/news/politics/2023-10-20/ty-article-magazine/.premium/0000018b-499a-dc3c-a5df-ddbaab290000, archived via https://archive.is/DMBwA.

32.    Ibid.

33.  Ruth Margalit, "Hadar Goldin and the Hannibal Directive," *The New Yorker*, August 6, 2014, accessed August 4, 2024, https://www.newyorker.com/news/news-desk/hadar-goldin-hannibal-directive.

34.  Amnesty International and Forensic Architecture, "'Black Friday': Carnage in Rafah During 2014 Israel/Gaza Conflict," *Amnesty International website*, July 2015, accessed August 4, 2024, https://blackfriday.amnesty.org.

35.  Ilan Pappé, *Lobbying for Zionism on Both Sides of the Atlantic*, (London: One World Publication, 2024), 248.

36.  Ibid., 250

37.  Ibid., 251

38.  Luke Broadwater, "AIPAC Demonstrates Its Clout With Defeat of a Second 'Squad' Member," *The New York Times*, August 7, 2024, accessed August 8, 2024, https://www.nytimes.com/2024/08/07/us/politics/bush-bell-aipac-missouri-primary.html.

39.  Elena Schneider and Melanie Mason, "AIPAC uncorks $100 million war chest to sink progressive candidates," *Politico*, March 3, 2024, accessed August 8, 2024, https://www.politico.com/news/2024/03/03/aipac-israel-spending-democratic-primaries-00144552.

40.  The Electronic Intifada, "Watch the Film the Israel Lobby Didn't Want You to See," *The Electronic Intifada*, November 2, 2018, accessed August 4, 2024, https://electronicintifada.net/content/watch-film-israel-lobby-didnt-want-you-see/25876.

41.  Reuters, "Key US Lawmakers Want to Boost Israel's $38 Billion Defense Aid Package." *Reuters*, February 27, 2018, accessed August 4, 2024, https://www.reuters.com/article/us-usa-israel-defense/key-u-s-lawmakers-want-to-boost-israels-38-billion-defense-aid-package-idUSKCN1GB2NQ/.

42.  Clayton Swisher, "We Made a Documentary Exposing the 'Israel Lobby.' Why Hasn't It Run?," *The Forward*, March 9, 2018. https://forward.com/opinion/396203/we-made-a-documentary-exposing-the-israel-lobby-why-hasnt-it-run/

43.  Facts.net, "50 Facts About Al Jazeera," *Facts.net*, September 24, 2024, accessed September 27, 2024, https://facts.net/culture-and-the-arts/mass-media/50-facts-about-al-jazeera/.

44.  Amir Tibon, "Qatar to US Jewish Leaders: Al Jazeera Israel Lobby Film Won't Air," Haaretz, February 8, 2018, archived at https://web.archive.org/web/20220616165206/https://www.haaretz.com/us-news/2018-02-08/ty-article/.premium/qatar-to-u-s-jewish-leaders-al-jazeera-israel-lobby-film-wont-air/0000017f-ef40-d0f7-a9ff-efc5fbad0000, accessed September 27, 2024.

45.  Jonathan Weisman, "Miriam Adelson Presses Trump on Moving US Embassy to Jerusalem," *The New York Times*, June 25, 2024, accessed September 30, 2024, https://www.nytimes.com/2024/06/25/us/politics/miriam-adelson-trump-israel.html.

46.  Indlieb Farazi Saber, "A 'Cultural Genocide': Which of Gaza's Heritage Sites Have Been Destroyed?," *Al Jazeera*, January 14,2024, accessed August 2, 2024, https://www.aljazeera.com/news/2024/1/14/a-cultural-genocide-which-of-gazas-heritage-sites-have-been-destroyed.

47.  Leanne Abraham, et al., "Israel's Controlled Demolitions Are Razing Neighborhoods in Gaza," *The New York Times*, February 3, 2024, accessed August 2, 2024, https://www.nytimes.com/interactive/2024/02/01/world/middleeast/Israel-gaza-war-demolish.html.

48.  Al Jazeera, "How Israel Has Destroyed Gaza's Schools and Universities," *Al Jazeera*, June 10, 2024, August 2, 2024, https://www.aljazeera.com/news/2024/1/24/how-israel-has-destroyed-gazas-schools-and-universities.

49.  Connie Hanzhang Jin, "War Has Forced Half of Gaza Into Rafah. Palestinians There Are at a Breaking Point," *NPR*, March 15, 2024, accessed August 3, 2024, https://www.npr.org/2024/03/15/1233158434/rafah-gaza-population-crowding-israel-hamas.

50.  Jason Burke, Aseel Mousa, and Malak A. Tantesh, "Al-Mawasi: Palestinians Fleeing to 'Humanitarian Zone' Find Little Hope," *The Guardian*, May 6, 2024, accessed 3, 2024,

https://www.theguardian.com/world/2024/mar/26/gaza-al-mawasi-palestinians-fleeing-to-humanitarian-zone-find-little-hope.

51.  Israel Defense Forces, "October 18, 2023 IDF Calls Residents of Gaza to Evacuate to Humanitarian Area in Al-Mawasi, Where International Humanitarian Aid Will Be Provided," October 18, 2023, accessed August 3, 2024, *IDF website*, https://www.idf.il/en/mini-sites/idf-press-releases-regarding-the-hamas-israel-war/october-23-pr/idf-calls-residents-of-gaza-to-evacuate-to-humanitarian-area-in-al-mawasi-where-international-humanitarian-aid-will-be-provided/

52.  Ismaeel Naar, "NGOs Call for Investigation Into Israeli Strike on Gazan Safe Zone in Al Mawasi," *The National*, March 14, 2024, accessed August 3, 2024, https://www.henationalnews.com/mena/palestine-israel/2024/03/14/ngos-call-for-investigation-into-an-israeli-strike-on-a-gazan-safe-zone-in-al-mawasi/.

53.  Médecins Sans Frontières (MSF) International, "MSF Strongly Condemns Deadly Israeli Attack on MSF Shelter in Gaza," *MSF website*, February 21, 2024, accessed August 3, 2024, https://www.msf.org/msf-strongly-condemns-deadly-israeli-attack-msf-shelter-gaza.

54.  Ben Van Der Merwe and Michelle Inez Simon, "The Price of Freedom: The Company Making Millions From Gaza's Misery," *Sky News*, March 1, 2024, accessed August 3, 2024, https://news.sky.com/story/the-price-of-freedom-the-company-making-millions-from-gazas-misery-13081454.

55.  Airwars, "Airwars assessment —incident code: ISPT0587," *Airwars*, July 9, 2024, accessed August 5, 2024, https://airwars.org/civilian-casualties/ispt0587-october-25-2023/.

56.  The New Arab Staff, "Israel has destroyed 1,000 of Gaza's 1,2000 mosques since 7 October, officials say," *The New Arab*, January 21, 2024, accessed August 5, 2024, https://www.newarab.com/news/israel-has-destroyed-1000-mosques-gaza-7-october.

57.  Euro-Med Human Rights Monitor, "200 days of military attack on Gaza: A horrific death toll amid intl. failure to stop Israel's genocide of Palestinians," *Euro-Med Monitor*, April 24, 2023, accessed August 5, 2024), https://euromedmonitor.org/en/article/6282/200-days-of-military-attack-on-Gaza:-A-horrific-death-toll-amid-intl.-failure-to-stop-Israel%E2%80%99s-genocide-of-Palestinians.

58.  An average of 10 children per day lost one or both of their legs to amputation since October 7, according to a report from the UN See World Health Organization, "Hostilities in the occupied Palestinian territory (oPt)—Public Health Situation Analysis (PHSA)," UN *website*, May 2, 2024, accessed August 1, 2024, https://www.un.org/unispal/wp-content/uploads/2024/05/WHO-PHSA-oPt-020524-FINAL.pdf.

59.  Rasha Khatib, Martin McKee, and Salim Yusuf, "Counting the Dead in Gaza: Difficult but Essential," *The Lancet*, July 5, 2024, accessed August 3, 2024, https://doi.org/10.1016/s0140-6736(24)01169-3.

60.  CARE Australia, "Birth under Bombs – 9 Months of Hell in Gaza," *CARE Australia*, July 10, 2024, accessed August 5, 2024, https://www.care.org.au/media/media-releases/birth-under-bombs-9-months-of-hell-in-gaza/.

61.  Ari Daniel, "Gaza Launches a Polio Vaccination Campaign amid Ongoing Conflict," *NPR*, September 13, 2024, accessed September 30, 2024, https://www.npr.org/sections/goats-and-soda/2024/09/13/g-s1-22620/gaza-polio-vaccination-campaign.

62.  Francesca Albanese, "Anatomy of a Genocide – Report of the Special Rapporteur on the situation of human rights in the Palestinian territory occupied since 1967 to Human Rights Council – Advance unedited version (A/HRC/55/73)," *United Nations Human Rights Council, UNISPAL*, March 26, 2024, accessed August 5, 2024, https://www.un.org/unispal/wp-content/uploads/2024/03/a-hrc-55-73-auv.pdf.

63.  Francesca Albanese, "Genocide as colonial erasure," Report of the Special Rapporteur on the situation of human rights in the Palestinian territory occupied since 1967,

United Nations General Assembly, October 1, 2024, accessed October 28, 2024, https://documents.un.org/doc/undoc/gen/n24/279/68/pdf.

64. Ibid.

65. Law for Palestine, "Database of Israeli Incitement to Genocide," Law for Palestine, January 15, 2024, accessed August 5, 2024, https://law4palestine.org/wp-content/uploads/2024/02/Database-of-Israeli-Incitement-to-Genocide-including-after-ICJ-order-27th-February-2024-.pdf.

66. *Application of the Convention on the Prevention and Punishment of the Crime of Genocide in the Gaza Strip (South Africa v. Israel)* (Application Instituting Proceedings and Request for Provisional Measures), ICJ Report, December 29, 2023, accessed September 27, 2024, https://www.icj-cij.org/sites/default/files/case-related/192/192-20231228-app-01-00-en.pdf.

67. Law for Palestine, "Database of Israeli Incitement to Genocide," Law for Palestine, January 15, 2024, https://law4palestine.org/wp-content/uploads/2024/02/Database-of-Israeli-Incitement-to-Genocide-including-after-ICJ-order-27th-February-2024-.pdf.

68. Ibid.

69. Ibid.

70. Ibid.

71. Nick Gillespie, "That Time Tom Friedman Said the Iraq War Was All About Telling Muslims 'To Suck. On. This.'," May 30, 2014, *Reason*, accessed September 27, 2024, https://reason.com/2014/05/30/that-time-tom-friedman-said-the-iraq-war/.

72. Al Jazeera, "Israel Says 'High Possibility' Its Army Killed Shireen Abu Akleh," *Al Jazeera*, May 25, 2023, accessed August 4, 2024, https://www.aljazeera.com/news/2022/9/5/israel-probe-shireen-abu-akleh.

73. *Democracy Now!*, "Rachel Corrie's Parents Mourn Death of Ayşenur Eygi, Warn of Israeli Military Cover-Up," Democracy Now!, September 9, 2024, accessed December 5, 2024, https://www.democracynow.org/2024/9/9/aysenur_eygi_rachel_corrie.

74. Jonathan Cook, "This is another Iraqi WMD moment. We are being gaslit," October 18, 2023, accessed September 27, 2024, *Jonathan Cook Blog*, https://www.jonathan-cook.net/blog/2023-10-18/ahli-hospital-gaza-gaslit/.

75. Amnesty International, "Unlawful and Deadly: Rocket and Mortar Attacks by Palestinian Armed Groups During the 2014 Gaza/Israel Conflict," *Amnesty International*, November 5, 2014, accessed December 5, 2024, https://www.amnesty.org/en/wp-content/uploads/2021/05/MDE2111782015ENGLISH.pdf.

76. George Orwell, *1984*, 5th ed, (London: Penguin Books, 2008), 37.

77. Gustave Le Bon, *The Crowd: A Study of the Popular Mind*, (Mineola, NY: Dover Publications, 2002), 67.

78. Hannah Arendt, *The Origins of Totalitarianism*, 2nd ed. (Cleveland: The World Publishing Company, 1968), 9.

79. Ibid., 9.

80. Jonathan Masters, "US Aid to Israel in Four Charts," Council on Foreign Relations, May 31, 2024, accessed August 6, 2024. https://www.cfr.org/article/us-aid-israel-four-charts.

81. John Mearsheimer and Stephen Walt, "The Israel Lobby," *London Review of Books* 28, no. 6, March 23, 2006, accessed September 27, 2024, https://www.lrb.co.uk/the-paper/v28/n06/john-mearsheimer/the-israel-lobby.

82. Thirty-three of the Israel-related resolutions vetoed by the US pertained to Israel's illegal occupations since 1967 and/or its treatment of the Palestinians with the remainder pertaining to its illegal invasions and occupations of Lebanon. In addition to these forty-five vetoed resolutions, a forty-sixth, proposed on April 17, 2023, would have recommended the UN. General Assembly accept Palestine as a member. See, Dag Hammarskjöld Library, "UN Security Council Meetings & Outcomes Tables: Security

Council—Veto List (in reverse chronological order)," *United Nations website*, accessed August 6, 2024, https://www.un.org/Depts/dhl/resguide/scact_veto_table_en.htm.

83. Mearsheimer and Walt, "The Israel Lobby."

84. International Justice Order. (2024, January 26). *Application of the Convention on the Prevention and Punishment of the Crime of Genocide in the Gaza Strip (South Africa v. Israel)* (Document No. 192-20240126-ORD-01-00-EN) [Order]. Case 192.

85. Ibid.

86. Ibid.

87. Yahoo News, "South Africa's Naledi Pandor speaks to the press about calls for a ceasefire in Gaza," *Yahoo News*, January 26, 2024, accessed September 27, 2024, https://uk.news.yahoo.com/south-africas-naledi-pandor-speaks-134041521.html.

88. Jewish Institute for National Security Affairs, "US Arms Transfers to Israel Since October 7," *JINSA website*, July 23, 2024, accessed August 6, 2024, https://jinsa.org/jinsa_report/infographic-u-s-arms-transfers-to-israel-since-october-7/.

89. Reuters and Times of Israel staff, "Who are Israel's key weapons suppliers, and who has halted exports since Oct. 7?," May 10, 2024, *The Times of Israel*, accessed August 6, 2024, https://www.timesofisrael.com/who-are-israels-key-weapons-suppliers-and-who-has-halted-exports-since-oct-7/.

90. Brett Murphy, "Israel Deliberately Blocked Humanitarian Aid to Gaza, Two Government Bodies Concluded. Antony Blinken Rejected Them.," *ProPublica*, September 24, 2024, accessed September 27, 2024, https://www.propublica.org/article/gaza-palestine-israel-blocked-humanitarian-aid-blinken.

91. Ibid.

92. Ibid.

93. "US Warns Israel over Gaza Aid Restrictions," *BBC News*, April 25, 2024, accessed October 2, 2024, https://www.bbc.co.uk/news/world-us-canada-68984999.

94. Reuters, "Reactions to World Court ruling on Israel's war in Gaza," *Reuters*, January 26, 2024, accessed September 27, 2024, https://www.reuters.com/world/reactions-world-court-ruling-israels-war-gaza-2024-01-26/.

95. The Times of Israel, "Ben Gvir slams ICJ as antisemitic, says Israel should ignore ruling on provisional measures," *The Times of Israel*, January 26, 2024, accessed September 27, 2024, https://www.timesofisrael.com/liveblog_entry/ben-gvir-slams-icj-as-antisemitic-says-israel-should-ignore-ruling-on-provisional-measures/.

96. Ibid.

97. Ibid, International Justice Order.

98. Ibid.

99. Ibid.

100. Ibid.

101. Ibid.

102. Benjamin Netanyahu, "Eulogy by PM Netanyahu for Eyal Yifrah, Gilad Sha'er and Naftali Frenkel," *Mission of Israel to the UN in Geneva*, July 1, 2014, accessed 1 August 2024, https://embassies.gov.il/UnGeneva/NewsAndEvents/Pages/Eulogy-by-PM-Netanyahu-for-Eyal-Yifrah-Gilad-Shaer-Naftali-Frenkel-1-Jul-2014.aspx.

103. Ibid, International Justice Order.

104. Sven Lindqvist, *Exterminate all the Brutes: One Man's Odyssey Into the Heart of Darkness and the Origins of European Genocide*, trans. Joan Tate, (New York: The New Press,1992), 8.

105. David Barsamian, *The Pen and the Sword: Conversations with Edward Said*, (Monroe, ME: Common Courage Press, 1994), 54.

106. Tia Goldenberg, "Harsh Israeli rhetoric against Palestinians becomes central to South Africa's genocide case," *The Associated Press*, January 18, 2024, accessed September 27,

2024, https://apnews.com/article/israel-palestinians-south-africa-genocide-hate-speech-97a9e4a84a3a6bebeddfb80f8a030724.

107. Sky News, "Energy Will Not Be Returned to the Territory Until Israeli Hostages Are Freed, Israel's Energy Minister Has Said," *Sky News,* October 12, 2023, accessed August 2, 2024, https://news.sky.com/video/were-fighting-nazis-former-israeli-prime-minister-defends-cutting-off-energy-to-gaza-strip-12983288.

108. Sarah Fortinsky, "Netanyahu Labels Hamas 'the New Nazis' alongside Germany's Scholz," *The Hill,* October 17, 2023, accessed August 2, 2024, https://thehill.com/policy/international/4261308-netanyahu-labels-hamas-the-new-nazis-alongside-germanys-scholz/.

109. Joseph Conrad, quoted in Sven Lindqvist, *Exterminate All the Brutes: One Man's Odyssey into the Heart of Darkness and the Origins of European Genocide,* trans. Joan Tate, (New York: The New Press,1996), 83.

110. Ilan Pappé, "Israel's righteous fury and its victims in Gaza," January 2, 2009, *The Electronic Intifada,* accessed August 4, 2024, https://electronicintifada.net/content/israels-righteous-fury-and-its-victims-gaza/7912.

111. Emanuel Fabian, "Israeli arms sales break record for 3rd year in row, reaching $13 billion in 2023," *The Times of Israel,* 17 June 2024, accessed August 4, 2024, https://www.timesofisrael.com/israeli-arms-sales-break-record-for-3rd-year-in-row-reaching-13-billion-in-2023/.

112. Margo Gutierrez and Milton Jamail, "Israel in Central America," *Middle East Research and Information Project,* May/June 1986, accessed August 3, 2024, https://merip.org/1986/05/israel-in-central-america/; Jo-Marie Burt and Paulo Estrada, "Legacy of Guatemala Dictator Ríos Montt Shows Justice is Possible" *Washington Office on Latin America,* April 13, 2018, accessed August 3, 2024, https://www.wola.org/analysis/legacy-guatemala-dictator-rios-montt-shows-justice-possible.

113. Yair Auron, "Revealing Israel's arms exports to perpetrators of genocide is a moral obligation" *Middle East Monitor,* July 3, 2017, accessed August 3, 2024, https://www.middleeastmonitor.com/20170703-concealing-israels-arms-exports-to-perpetrators-of-genocide-is-a-moral-obligation/.

114. Antony Loewenstein, *The Palestine Laboratory: How Israel Exports the Technology of Occupation Around the World,* (London: Verso Books, 2023), 100.

115. Ibid., 139.

116. Ibid., 99.

117. John Scott-Railton, Bill Marczak, Siena Anstis, Bahr Abdul Razzak, Masashi Crete-Nishihata, and Ron Deibert, "Wife of Journalist Slain in Cartel-Linked Killing Targeted with NSO Group's Spyware," *The Citizen Lab,* March 20, 2019, accessed August 4, 2024, https://citizenlab.ca/2019/03/nso-spyware-slain-journalists-wife/. See also, John Scott-Railton, Bill Marczak, Bahr Abdul Razzak, Siena Anstis, Paolo Nigro Herrero, and Ron Deibert, "New Pegasus Spyware Abuses Identified in Mexico," *The Citizen Lab,* October 2, 2022, accessed August 4, 2024, https://citizenlab.ca/2022/10/new-pegasus-spyware-abuses-identified-in-mexico/.

118. Stephanie Kirchgaessner, "Saudis Behind NSO Spyware Attack on Jamal Khashoggi's Family, Leak Suggests," *The Guardian,* July 18, 2021, accessed August 4, 2024, https://www.theguardian.com/world/2021/jul/18/nso-spyware-used-to-target-family-of-jamal-khashoggi-leaked-data-shows-saudis-pegasus.

119. Matt Kennard, "The Cruel Experiments of Israel's Arms Industry," *The Electronic Intifada,* December 27, 2016, accessed August 4, 2024, https://electronicintifada.net/content/cruel-experiments-israels-arms-industry/19011.

120. Rania Khalek, "St. Louis Police Bought Israeli Skunk Spray After Ferguson Uprising," *The Electronic Intifada,* August 13, 2015, accessed August 4, 2024, https://

electronicintifada.net/blogs/rania-khalek/st-louis-police-bought-israeli-skunk-spray-after-ferguson-uprising.

121. Ibid.
122. Amnesty International, "Automated Apartheid: The Use of Facial Recognition Technology in Palestinian Territories Occupied by Israel," *Amnesty International*, May 2, 2023, accessed December 5, 2024, https://www.amnesty.org/en/documents/mde15/6701/2023/en/.
123. Disclose, "The French National Police is Unlawfully Using an Israeli Facial Recognition Software," *Disclose*, November 14, 2023, accessed December 5, 2024, https://disclose.ngo/en/article/the-french-national-police-is-unlawfully-using-an-israeli-facial-recognition-software.
124. Jeff Halper, *War Against the People* (London: Pluto Press, 2015), 109.
125. Tom Sperlinger, "How Does Israel Get Away With It?," *The Electronic Intifada*, October 2, 2015, accessed August 4, 2024, https://electronicintifada.net/content/how-does-israel-get-away-it/14882.
126. Antony Loewenstein, *The Palestine Laboratory: How Israel Exports the Technology of Occupation Around the World* (London: Verso Books, 2023), 59.
127. David Rosenberg, "To be a Jew means always being with the oppressed, never with the oppressors," *Jewish Voice for Labour*, September 26, 2017, accessed October 2, 2024, https://www.jewishvoiceforlabour.org.uk/article/jew-means-always-oppressed-never-oppressors/.
128. Rashid Khalidi, *The Hundred Years' War on Palestine: A History of Settler Colonialism and Resistance, 1917-2017*, (Metropolitan Books: New York, 2020).
129. Lorenzo Kamel, *Imperial Perceptions of Palestine: British Influence and Power in Late Ottoman Times*, (I.B. Tauris: Croydon, 2015), 95.
130. Secretary of State for India Edwin Montagu, "The Anti-Semitism of the Present Government," The National Archive of the UK, 23 August 1917, CAB 24/24/71. For an easily accessible version of memo Montagu sent to his fellow cabinet members, see Balfour Project, "Memorandum of Edwin Montagu on the Anti-Semitism of the Present (British) Government," *Balfour Project website*, accessed at August 2, 2024, https://balfourproject.org/edwin-montagu-and-zionism-1917/.
131. Vladimir Ze'ev Jabotinsky, "The Iron Wall", trans. from Russian, *Jabotinsky Institute in Israel*, November 4, 1923, accessed August 1, 2024, https://en.jabotinsky.org/media/9747/the-iron-wall.pdf.
132. Rashid Khalidi, *The Hundred Years' War on Palestine: A History of Settler Colonialism and Resistance*, 1917-2017, (New York: Metropolitan Books, 2020), 16–17.
133. Ibid., 17.
134. Ibid., 17.
135. Ibid., 18.
136. Ibid., 105.
137. Ibid., 38.
138. Uri Avnery, "Weimar in Jerusalem: the rise of fascism in Israel," *Redress Information and Analysis*, Oct 23, 2010, accessed August 2, 2024, https://www.redressonline.com/2010/10/the-rise-of-fascism-in-israel/.
139. Al Mayadeen English, "Nearly half a million Israelis left occupied Palestine since October 7," *Al Mayadeen*, December 6, 2023, accessed August 4, 2024, https://english.almayadeen.net/news/politics/nearly-half-a-million-israelis-left-occupied-palestine-since.
140. Patrick Kingsley and Bilal Shbair, "Inside the Base Where Israel Has Detained Thousands of Gazans," *The New York Times*, June 6, 2024, accessed August 4, 2024, https://www.nytimes.com/2024/06/06/world/middleeast/israel-gaza-detention-base.html.

141. Fadi Baker, testimony given to B'Tselem, as part of "Welcome to Hell: The Israeli Prison System as a Network of Torture Camps," *B'Tselem*, August 2024, accessed August 7, 2024, https://www.btselem.org/publications/202408_welcome_to_hell/testimony_of_fadi_baker.
142. Ibid.
143. Ibid.
144. Ibid.
145. Max Blumenthal, *Goliath: Life and Loathing in Greater Israel*, (New York: Nation Books, 2013), 264.
146. Yeshayahu Leibowitz, *Judaism, Human Values, and the Jewish State*, (Harvard University Press, 1992), 224.
147. Ibid., 22-226.
148. Tacitus, *Annals*, trans. Cynthia Damon, (London: Penguin Classics, 2012), 325.
149. The title and concept of Nero's Guests comes from a lecture by P. Sainath about the suicides of Indian farmers.
150. Abraham Joshua Heschel, *The Prophets*, Harper Perennial Classics ed., (New York: Harper Perennial, 2001), 364-365.
151. Doctors Without Borders / Médecins Sans Frontières "Gaza: Patients and Medical Staff Trapped in Hospitals Under Fire," *MSF website*, November 20, 2023, accessed August 3, 2024. https://www.doctorswithoutborders.ca/patients-medical-staff-trapped-in-hospitals-under-fire/.
152. World Health Organization, "WHO analysis highlights vast unmet rehabilitation needs in Gaza," *WHO website*, September 12, 2024, accessed September 27, 2024, https://www.un.org/unispal/wp-content/uploads/2024/05/WHO-PHSA-oPt-020524-FINAL.pdf.
153. Matt Stieb, "What We Know About Aaron Bushnell's Self-Immolation," *New York Magazine*, January 9, 2023, accessed September 27, 2024, https://nymag.com/intelligencer/article/aaron-bushnell-self-immolation-what-we-know.html.
154. Walter Benjamin, "Critique of Violence," in *Reflections: Essays, Aphorisms, and Autobiographical Writings*, (New York: Schocken Books, 1978), 277-300.
155. Ibid., 300.
156. Walter Benjamin, "Goethe's Elective Affinities," in *Selected Writings, Volume 1, 1913-1926*, (Belknap Press, 1996), 356.
157. Raul Hilberg, *The Destruction of the European Jews, Vol. I, II, III*, 3rd ed., (New Haven: Yale University Press, 2003), 88.
158. Ibid., 53.
159. Primo Levi, *The Drowned and the Saved*, trans. Raymond Rosenthal, (London: Michael Joseph, Penguin Group, 1988), 18.
160. Ibid., 22.
161. Ibid., 50-51.
162. Ibid., 23.
163. Primo Levi, "The Gray Zone," In *The Holocaust: Origins, Implementation, Aftermath*, ed. Omer Bartov, 251-272, (Routledge: 2001), 255.
164. Primo Levi, *Moments of Reprieve*, trans. Ruth Feldman, (New York: Penguin, 1987), 127.
165. Christopher R. Browning, *Ordinary Men*, (New York: HarperPerennial,1992), 223.
166. Ilan Pappé, "Israel, the Holocaust and the Nakba," *Socialist Review*, May 1, 2008, accessed August 2, 2024, https://socialistworker.co.uk/socialist-review-archive/israel-holocaust-and-nakba/.
167. Thích Nhất Hạnh, *Vietnam: Lotus in a Sea of Fire*, (New York: Hill and Wang, 1967), 106-107.
168. Reinhold Niebuhr, *Moral Man and Immoral Society*, (New York: Charles Scribner's Sons, 1960), 277.
169. Reinhold Niebuhr, "The Twilight of Liberalism," *New Republic*, June 14, 1919.

170. Daniel Berrigan, *The Trial of the Catonsville Nine*, (Boston: Beacon Press, 1970), 91-92.

171. Gillian Goodman, "Columbia's Most Recent Arrests Had Almost No Observers. Here's What I Saw and What We Know," *Prism*, May 8, 2024, accessed August 4, 2024, https://prismreports.org/2024/05/07/heres-what-we-know-about-most-recent-arrests-at-columbia.

172. Brett Wilkins, "Missing 6-Year-Old Gaza Girl Hind Rajab Found Dead With Massacred Family, Rescue Workers," *Common Dreams*, February 10, 2024, accessed August 4, 2024, https://www.commondreams.org/news/hind-rajab, see also Alexander Bolton, "Schumer Condemns 'Lawlessness' at Columbia University Protests," *The Hill*, April 30, 2024, accessed August 4, 2024, https://thehill.com/homenews/senate/4633779-schumer-columbia-protests/.

173. Sravya Tadepalli, "Pro-Palestine Students at Columbia University Speak Out About 'Skunk' Attack," *Prism*, January 30, 2024, accessed August 4, 2024, https://prismreports.org/2024/01/30/pro-palestine-students-at-columbia-university-speak-out-about-skunk-attack/.

174. Gaby Del Valle, "Columbia University Has a Doxxing Problem," *The Verge*, April 26, 2024, accessed August 4, 2024, https://www.theverge.com/24141073/columbia-doxxing-truck-student-encampment-palestine-israel.

175. Nadda Osman, "Israel Broadcasts Baby Sounds to 'Lure Palestinians' in Gaza," *The New Arab*, April 17, 2024, accessed August 4, 2024, https://www.newarab.com/news/israel-broadcasts-baby-sounds-lure-palestinians-gaza.

176. United Nations Regional Information Centre for Western Europe, "The UN and the Crisis in Gaza: What You Need to Know," *UNRIC website*, last modified September 30, 2024, accessed September 30, 2024, https://unric.org/en/the-un-and-the-crisis-in-the-middle-east-gaza/.

# APPENDIX

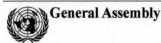

United Nations

A/79/384

## General Assembly

Distr.: General
1 October 2024

Original: English

**Seventy-ninth session**
Item 71 (c) of the provisional agenda*
**Promotion and protection of human rights: human
rights situations and reports of special rapporteurs
and representatives**

### Situation of human rights in the Palestinian territories occupied since 1967**

#### Note by the Secretary-General

The Secretary-General has the honour to transmit to the General Assembly the report of the Special Rapporteur on the situation of human rights in the Palestinian territories occupied since 1967, Francesca Albanese, in accordance with Human Rights Council resolution 5/1.

---

* A/79/150.
** The present report was submitted after the deadline in order to reflect the most recent information.

24-17834 (E)    221024
*2417834*

Please recycle

A/79/384

## Report of the Special Rapporteur on the situation of human rights in the Palestinian territories occupied since 1967, Francesca Albanese

### Genocide as colonial erasure

*Summary*

In the present report, the Special Rapporteur on the situation of human rights in the Palestinian territories occupied since 1967, Francesca Albanese, examines the unfolding horrors in the occupied Palestinian territory. While the wholesale destruction of Gaza continues unabated, other parts of the land have not been spared. The violence that Israel has unleashed against the Palestinians post-7 October is not happening in a vacuum, but is part of a long-term intentional, systematic, State-organized forced displacement and replacement of the Palestinians. This trajectory risks causing irreparable prejudice to the very existence of the Palestinian people in Palestine. Member States must intervene now to prevent new atrocities that will further scar human history.

24-17834

# I. Introduction

1. In March 2024, the Special Rapporteur on the situation of human rights in the Palestinian territory occupied since 1967, Francesca Albanese, concluded that there were reasonable grounds to believe that Israel had committed acts of genocide in Gaza. In the present report, the Special Rapporteur expands the analysis of the post- 7 October 2023 violence against Gaza, which has spread to the West Bank, including East Jerusalem. She focuses on genocidal intent, contextualising the situation within a decades-long process of territorial expansion and ethnic cleansing aimed at liquidating the Palestinian presence in Palestine. She suggests that genocide should be seen as integral and instrumental to the aim of full Israeli colonization of Palestinian land while removing as many Palestinians as possible.

2. The present report is based on legal research and analysis, interviews with victims and witnesses, including in Jordan and Egypt, open-source information and input from experts and civil-society organizations. The Special Rapporteur, still refused access to the occupied Palestinian territory, stresses that Israel has no authority to bar fact-finding mechanisms from the territory that it illegally occupies. The persistent denial of access to United Nations mechanisms and investigators of the International Criminal Court (ICC) may constitute obstruction of justice, in defiance of the International Court of Justice (ICJ) order that Israel allow international investigators to enter Gaza and take measures to ensure the preservation of evidence.

3. While the scale and nature of the ongoing Israeli assault against the Palestinians vary by area, the totality of the Israeli acts of destruction directed against the totality of the Palestinian people, with the aim of conquering the totality of the land of Palestine, is clearly identifiable. Patterns of violence against the group as a whole warrant the application of the Convention on the Prevention and Punishment of the Crime of Genocide (Genocide Convention) in order to cease, prevent and punish genocide in the whole of the occupied Palestinian territory.

## II.  Legal framework and developments

4.  In the present report, the Special Rapporteur relies on the legal framework considered in previous reports, including international humanitarian law, international human rights law, international criminal law and customary international law, in particular the Genocide Convention and the International Convention on the Suppression and Punishment of the Crime of Apartheid, together with relevant legal developments and jurisprudence.

5.  Two important legal developments informed the present report. First, in its Advisory Opinion of July 2024, ICJ declared the prolonged presence of Israel in the whole of the Palestinian territory occupied since 1967, including its colony regime, as unlawful and aimed at annexation. It stated that Israeli annexation was designed to be permanent, creating "irreversible effects on the ground", "undermin[ing] the integrity of the Palestinian people in the Occupied Palestinian Territory" and seeking to "acquire sovereignty over an occupied territory".

6.  The Court recognized the violation of non-derogable norms prohibiting territorial acquisition by force, racial segregation and apartheid, and protecting the right to self-determination of the Palestinian people, concluding that the occupation constitutes an act of aggression, in all but name, deriving in part from its settler- colonial nature. It stressed the obligation to rapidly end the occupation, dismantle and evacuate the colonies, provide full reparation to Palestinian victims and allow the return of Palestinians displaced since 1967.

7.  Expanding on the *Wall* opinion, the Court rejected arguments that Israeli "security concerns" justify the occupation. The declared unlawfulness of the occupation vitiates claims of purported self-defence; the only lawful recourse available to Israel is its unconditional withdrawal from the whole of that territory.

8.  Second, in *South Africa v. Israel*, the Court ordered provisional measures to prevent and/or stop acts of genocide. After recognizing, in January 2024, the existence of a "real and imminent risk [of] irreparable prejudice" to the rights of the Palestinians in Gaza under the Genocide Convention, the Court instructed Israel to "prevent the commission of all acts"

outlined in the Convention. In March, the Court took notice of the worsening humanitarian crisis, and in May, recognizing an "exceptionally grave" risk in Rafah, it ordered Israel to "immediately halt its military offensive". Despite this, Israel, and most other States, continue to disregard such orders, with arms continuing to flow to Israel.

# III. The unfolding genocide as a "means to an end"

9. On 14 October 2023, after Israel ordered 1.1 million Palestinians to move south from northern Gaza in 24 hours – "one of the fastest mass displacements in history" – the Special Rapporteur warned of the risk of deliberate mass ethnic cleansing. This proved prescient. At least 90 per cent of Palestinians in Gaza have now been forcibly displaced – many more than 10 times – amid calls from Israeli officials and others for Palestinians to leave and Israelis to "return to Gaza" and rebuild the colonies dismantled in 2005.

10. Meanwhile, violence has spread beyond Gaza, with Israeli forces and violent settlers having escalated patterns of ethnic cleansing and apartheid in the West Bank, including East Jerusalem.

11. High-ranking Israeli officials, ministers and religious leaders continue to encourage erasure and dispossession of Palestinians, setting new thresholds for acceptable violence against civilians. The Nakba, which has been ongoing since 1948, has been deliberately accelerated.

12. In the following sections, the Special Rapporteur examines critical developments on the ground, highlighting patterns of conduct that evidence an intent to employ genocidal acts as a means to ethnically cleanse all or parts of the occupied Palestinian territory.

## A. Failure to cease and punish genocide in Gaza

13. Since the previous report of the Special Rapporteur (A/78/545), and despite the ICJ interventions, genocidal acts have proliferated. Nearly a year of scorched-earth assault has led to the calculated destruction of Gaza: the human, material and environmental cost is unquantifiable.

14. Since March 2024, Israel has killed 10,037 Palestinians and injured 21,767, with more than 93 massacres, bringing the reported totals to nearly 42,000 and 96,000 respectively, although figures from reliable sources are incomplete and may understate the magnitude of the casualties. Aid distribution sites, tents, hospitals, schools and markets have been repeatedly attacked through the indiscriminate use of aerial and sniper fire. At least 13,000 children, including more than 700 babies, have been killed, many shot in the head and chest. Approximately 22,500 Palestinians have sustained life-changing injuries. By May, a further 10,000 people were estimated to be buried under the rubble, including 4,000 children; the voices of those trapped and dying are often audible. An uncertain number are forcibly disappeared by Israeli forces.

15. The magnitude of destruction in Gaza has prompted allegations of domicide, urbicide, scholasticide, medicide, cultural genocide and ecocide. Nearly 40 million tons of debris, including unexploded ordnance and human remains, contaminate the ecosystem. More than 140 temporary waste sites and 340,000 tons of waste, untreated wastewater and sewage overflow contribute to the spread of diseases such as hepatitis A, respiratory infections, diarrhoea and skin diseases. As Israeli leaders promised, Gaza has been made unfit for human life.

16. Continued bombardment of evacuees in purportedly designated "safe zones" has continued to create hardship, terror and death. Displaced people have been systematically chased down and targeted in shelters, including in United Nations Relief and Works Agency for Palestine Refugees in the Near East (UNRWA) schools, 70 per cent of which Israel has repeatedly attacked. The Rafah offensive in May caused more than 3,500 direct deaths and new displacement of almost 1 million Palestinians to uninhabitable wastelands of rubble, sewage and decomposing bodies.

17. According to satellite imagery and other sources, Israeli soldiers have built roads and military bases in more than 26 per cent of Gaza, suggesting the aim of a permanent presence. The Israeli military expanded the "buffer zone" along the Gaza perimeter to 16 per cent of the territory, flattening homes, apartment blocks and agricultural farms. By August 2024, repeated evacuation orders over approximately 84

per cent of Gaza had corralled the majority of the population into a shrinking, unsafe "humanitarian zone" covering 12.6 per cent of a territory now reconfigured in preparation for annexation. In early September, two ministers of the Government of Israel openly called for the conquest and annexation of significant areas of Gaza.

18. Israel has continued to use "medical shielding" arguments to target healthcare facilities. According to the World Health Organization (WHO), in 300 days, 32 out of 36 hospitals were damaged, with 20 hospitals and 70 out of 119 primary healthcare centres incapacitated. By 20 August, Israel had attacked healthcare facilities 492 times. From 18 March to 1 April, Israeli forces again laid siege to Al-Shifa Hospital, killing more than 400 and detaining 300 people, including doctors, patients, displaced persons and civil servants. On 26 August, following mass expulsion orders in Deir al-Balah, where 1 million Palestinians were sheltering, Israeli forces compelled the evacuation of all but 100 of 650 patients in Al-Aqsa hospital. On 30 August, Israeli forces bombed a humanitarian truck bound for the Emirati hospital in Rafah, killing several aid workers.

19. On 16 July 2024, WHO detected the first presence of poliovirus in 25 years – a direct consequence of the destruction of water and sewage systems, obstruction of aid and shelter overcrowding. By late August, a 10-month-old baby was partially paralysed by the disease. Despite the looming outbreak, Israel delayed vaccinations and attacked vaccination areas and a United Nations vaccination convoy. While humanitarian organizations called for a ceasefire, Israel issued the highest number of evacuation orders since 13 October 2023, targeting areas with the highest concentration of displaced Palestinians, forcing the United Nations to suspend humanitarian operations.

20. Systematic attacks on Gaza food sovereignty indicate an intent to destroy its population through starvation. Israel has destroyed agricultural land and reservoirs and attacked distribution centres, coordination teams and aid convoys. Hungry crowds waiting for food have been massacred. Following constant evacuation orders and the Israeli takeover of the Rafah crossing, distribution of daily meals fell by 35 per cent from July to August 2024. In August, entry permits for

humanitarian organizations nearly halved. Access to water has been restricted to a quarter of pre-7 October levels. Approximately 93 per cent of the agricultural, forestry and fishing economies has been destroyed; 95 per cent of Palestinians face high levels of acute food insecurity, and deprivation for decades to come.

21. In August 2024, the Finance Minister of Israel, Bezalel Smotrich, stated that starving the entire Gaza population was "justified and moral", even if 2 million people consequently died. In recent months, 83 per cent of food aid was prevented from entering Gaza, and the civilian police in Rafah were repeatedly targeted, impairing distribution. At least 34 deaths from malnutrition were recorded by 14 September 2024. At the time of writing, the Prime Minister, Benjamin Netanyahu, was evaluating a plan to block all food supplies to northern Gaza proposed by adviser Giora Eiland, who previously endorsed introducing epidemics as a military tactic. The killing of civilian police and clan leadership providing security for food distribution further compounded the crisis across Gaza. Starvation and deprivation tactics in the north have been particularly egregious.

22. Palestinians have been systematically abused in a network of Israeli torture camps. Thousands have disappeared, many after being detained in appalling conditions, often bound to beds, blindfolded and in diapers, deprived of medical treatment and subjected to unsanitary conditions, starvation, torturous cuffing, severe beatings, electrocution and sexual assault by both humans and animals. At least 48 detainees have died in custody.

23. Even when conservatively considered, these multiple torments constitute precisely the irreparable harm that ICJ has warned against since January 2024, and which Israel has intentionally inflicted on the Palestinians as a group.

## A.  Risk of genocide in the West Bank, including East Jerusalem

24. The devastation inflicted on Gaza is now metastasizing to the West Bank, including East Jerusalem. In December 2023, the Defence Minister of Israel, Yoav Gallant, predicted that "when what the IDF did in Gaza becomes clear, that will also be projected on Judea and Samaria [West Bank]".

25. From 7 October 2023 to the end of September 2024, Israe-li forces carried out more than 5,505 raids. Violent settlers, supported by Israeli forces and officials, conducted 1,084 attacks, killing more than 692 Palestinians – 10 times the previous 14 years' annual average of 69 fatalities – and injuring 5,199.

26. The pattern of targeting children is shocking. Since 7 October, 169 Palestinian children have been killed, nearly 80 per cent of whom were shot in the head or torso. This represents a 250 per cent increase on the previous nine months, totalling more than 20 per cent of children killed in the West Bank since 2000.

27. Echoing the brutality that swept Gaza, Palestinians in the West Bank have been subjected to appalling detention practices, following orders by the National Security Minister of Israel, Itamar Ben-Gvir. A mass arrest campaign led to the detention of tens of thousands, with 9,400 currently detained. As in Gaza, many are academics, students, lawyers, journalists and human rights defenders, designated as "terrorists" or "national security threats". Leaked videos and interviews with prison officials revealed intentional and systemic abuse and brutality, degradation, torture and even rape. At least 12 detainees from the West Bank died as a result of torture and denial of medical care.

28. In November 2023, Bezalel Smotrich, "Governor of Judea and Samaria" and staunch advocate of colonization and mass expulsion, claimed that there are "2 million Nazis" in the West Bank. He then promised to turn several areas of the West Bank into a "pile of rubble like … [Gaza]". On 18 August, the Foreign Minister of Israel, Israel Katz, called for the West Bank to receive the same treatment as Gaza.

29. The northern West Bank has been the subject of particularly severe military violence. Protracted sieges, relentless raids and a major escalation since August 2024, including aerial bombardment, have wrought devastation. Forty- six drone and air strike operations killed 77 Palestinians, including 14 children. In Jenin camp approximately 180 homes were levelled and 3,800 structures damaged, destroying or damaging power supplies, public services and amenities, displacing thousands of families and causing widespread disruption. More than 181,000 Palestinians have been affected, many multiple times.

30. On 27 August 2024, Israeli forces launched operation "Summer Camps" against Jenin, Nablus, Qalqilya, Tubas and Tulkarem, fulfilling the promise to treat the West Bank like Gaza. For days on end, thousands were placed under curfew, without food or water. Israeli forces targeted ambulances, blocked entrances to hospitals and laid siege to Jenin Hospital. Bulldozers destroyed streets and electricity and public health infrastructure. Hundreds lost their homes and property; more than 1,000 families in Jenin were displaced. Thirty-six were killed, including eight children.

31. Targeted attacks on the health sector have been replicated in the West Bank. Medical workers and infrastructure were attacked 538 times, killing 23 people and injuring 100 and damaging 54 medical facilities, 20 mobile clinics and 374 ambulances, while critical medical care was impeded. Permits for Palestinians to access medical care outside the West Bank sharply declined.

32. On 29 May 2024, governance of the West Bank was officially transferred from military to civilian authorities – furthering *de jure* annexation – and placed under Bezalel Smotrich, a committed Eretz Yisrael politician. The largest single land appropriation in 30 years was then approved. Since 7 October, Israel has demolished, confiscated or ordered the demolition of more than 1,416 Palestinian structures, displacing more than 3,200 Palestinians, including approximately 1,400 children. At least 18 communities were depopulated under the threat of lethal force, effectively enabling the colonization of large tracts of Area C. This constitutes an escalation of unlawful conduct already found to be "aimed at dispersing the [Palestinian] population and undermining its integrity as a people".

33. The crippling of the economy is another existential threat. Amid extreme insecurity and fear, the suspension of financial transfers to the Palestinian Authority, the revocation of 148,000 work permits and severe movement restrictions, the gross domestic product (GDP) of the West Bank contracted by 22.7 per cent, nearly 30 per cent of businesses have closed, and 292,000 jobs have been lost.

34. Genocidal conduct in Gaza set an ominous precedent for the West Bank. The deliberate strategy of Israel to render Palestinian life unsustainable has markedly intensified everywhere in the occupied Palestinian territory, with devastating consequences for Palestinian survival.

# IV.  Understanding the legal complexity and scope of genocidal intent

35. Following the harrowing experience of recent genocides in Rwanda, the former Yugoslavia and, plausibly, Myanmar, what constitutes genocide in law – the destruction of a national, ethnical, racial or religious group, in whole or in part, as such – has become better established. However, preventing and punishing genocide in practice, in particular proving genocidal intent, is still developing.

36. The stigma attached to and the consequences of the crime of genocide often deter perpetrators from recording policies, plans and other indications of intent to carry it out (e.g. in writing). When direct evidence of intent is unavailable, inferring intent requires a complex assessment of facts, statements and circumstances. These factors should be borne in mind:

    a) While recognizing the possible composite nature of genocide is critical to its identification and prevention, the compartmentalization of the conduct into its disparate acts without recourse to broader context can obscure the requisite genocidal intent;

    b) Aside from the five acts that may constitute genocidal conduct, other acts can be indicative of genocidal intent;

    c) The existing jurisprudence has arisen primarily from the criminal prosecution of individuals; this can limit the early recognition of broader State responsibility for genocide, which is crucial to its prevention.

37. Understanding how the intent to destroy manifests – its relationship to the prescribed genocidal acts and the nature and scale of atrocities – is key when identifying conduct that could constitute evidence of genocidal intent as the only reasonable inference.

38. In the following sections, the Special Rapporteur briefly outlines how relevant jurisprudence, analysed *in abstracto*, is fully capable of capturing genocidal intent in State conduct when a comprehensive interpretative approach is adopted.

## A. Considering the plurality of facts, circumstances and conduct

39. The magnitude and complexity of the crime of genocide require close analysis of the genocidal conduct as a whole, properly situated in its broader context. Due consideration should be given to:

    • The destruction caused by the nature and scale of atrocities

    • The fog of war

    • Claims to retribution or alternative motives

    • The opportunity to commit genocide

40. In international practice, the same facts can form the basis of multiple charges (and constitute a war crime or crime against humanity and an act of genocide). When determining genocidal intent, it is critical to assess "whether all of the evidence, taken together, demonstrate[s] a genocidal mental state".

41. As observed by Judge Trindade in *Croatia v. Serbia*, an "onslaught of civilians" is not merely a "plurality of common crimes", but rather a "plurality of atrocities, which, in itself, by its extreme violence and devastation, can disclose the intent to destroy". The focus should be on whether all the acts – e.g. starvation, torture, killing, forced displacement, extermination – considered together in their totality form a pattern of conduct indicative of genocidal intent.

## B. Singularity of intent: destroying "a group" "as such"

42. In proving intent to destroy the group, all relevant factors must be examined holistically. Jurisprudence on genocidal intent is typically focused on "physical or biological destruction" of the group. The fact that the Genocide Convention was drafted when colonialism still played a significant role in international relations, and the vivid horror of the Holocaust's industrial-scale extermination, may account for the focus on physical and biological destruction over social and cultural factors. However, genocide is not a crime only of mass killing, as specified in the Convention itself. The genocidal act of "forcibly transferring children of the group to another group", for example, entails no killing at all.

43. Genocide is more structurally complex and insidious, and therefore more difficult to ascertain than crimes such as mass killing or extermination. A wider lens is required to identify the intent to destroy a group in whole or in part as such. International jurisprudence provides that acts other than the five listed in the Convention may be relevant evidence of genocidal intent. Accordingly, the historical and sociopolitical context in which genocide occurs is key to identifying how intent forms, and then materializes also through these other acts.

44. Jurisprudence has been broadly focused on determining intent through acts targeting "the very foundation of the group", including the imposition of living conditions leading to "slow death" and "the destruction of the spirit, of the will to live, and of life itself". In other words, intent to destroy is assessed holistically and in totality.

45. Jurisprudence has also recognized that a group is "comprised of its individuals, but also of its history, traditions, the relationship between its members, the relationship with other groups, the relationship with the land". Violent destruction of any of these components has a profound impact on the group and its ability to survive. Trauma, poverty, food scarcity, forced displacement, loss of homes, land and cultural heritage – and settler-colonialism as an "enduring structure" – are widely recognized determinants of individual and societal health.

46. In settler-colonial contexts, land and its resources are particularly relevant. Land is intrinsic to both a people's right to self-determination and the settler-colonial project. An inherent conflict exists between the colonizers, who seek to acquire and control the land, and the Indigenous population, for whom the land is integral to their identity: "where they are is who they are". Disconnection from land and cultural roots contributes to the erosion of identity and community resilience, resulting in physically destructive outcomes: poorer health, lower life expectancy and abnormally high suicide rates. The issue of land is therefore indicative of how the settler- colonial project destroys – in order to replace – the Indigenous population.

47. Consequently, components of conduct, such as repeated forced displacement, that result in the disconnection from

the land, as well as the destruction of the cultural, educational and economic structures that tie a people to the land, must be considered "significant as indicative of the presence of a specific intent … inspiring [other genocidal] acts". Forced displacement itself, together with aggravating factors – e.g. displacement into dangerous, squalid or toxic conditions – can constitute an underlying genocidal act. The particular vulnerability of the group must also be considered.

48. In short, intent to destroy has become established as the targeting of a group's existence such that "the group can no longer reconstitute itself".

## C. Genocidal intent in the context of State responsibility

49. Early identification of genocide is crucial to prevent genocide, ensuring that a central tenet of the post-Second World War international legal system is not a dead letter.

50. In assessing State responsibility for genocide – i.e. genocidal intent attributable to the State – ICJ has drawn heavily on the jurisprudence of international criminal tribunals. While acknowledging that State responsibility can be established "without an individual being convicted of the crime", in *Bosnia v. Serbia* in 2007, the Court found State genocidal intent only where individual perpetrators had been held criminally responsible. The Court established that, in the absence of direct evidence of State intent, the pattern of conduct must be such that it "could only point to the existence of such intent". This approach was tempered in 2015, in *Croatia v. Serbia*, where the Court determined that "reasonableness" must be considered when inferring genocidal intent from patterns of conduct.

51. However, further clarity is needed regarding genocidal intent in the context of State responsibility. State intent can be derived from the aggregate of individual perpetrators' genocidal intents, but States should not be exonerated simply because there are no individual criminal convictions, which, if they do occur, may come too late to prevent or stop genocide. While ICJ acknowledged that State obligations concerning genocide are "not of a criminal nature", the standard of proof required to ground the responsibility of a

State is a quasi-criminal standard. Among other things, this would delay or frustrate justice for victims.

52. Intervening in *The Gambia v. Myanmar*, currently before ICJ, six Western States argued that the "reasonableness criterion" requires a "balanced approach" so as not to make it "impossible" to determine genocidal intent "by way of inference" in other words, urging the Court not to miss the forest for the trees. Otherwise, this risks protecting the State over the victims that the Convention is designed to protect.

53. Three factors help achieve this balance:

(a) Applying the "only reasonable inference" test involves first filtering out other possible intents that could be inferred but are not reasonably supported by the evidence. A balanced consideration of the interplay between motives and intent should determine whether motives "preclude such a specific intent" to destroy a people, or whether they are consistent with, or even confirm, genocidal intent as the only reasonable inference;

(b) International law treats the State as a unit, not as separate organs. This means that conduct and intent of the State must be considered holistically. A rule of law-regulated State must be viewed as a whole, including its Government, parliament and judiciary and their regulatory functions;

(c) Given the high threshold set for establishing genocidal intent, the failure to illuminate the totality of conduct invites the possibility of invisibilizing the crime itself behind the claimed strategies, policies and actions that are advanced by the wrongdoing State in order to obscure it. Failure to recognize genocide in its totality may help create the camouflage that a State could employ to commit it.

# V.   "Totality triple lens": Israeli intent towards the Palestinians as a group as such

54. The current intent to destroy the people as such could not be more evident from Israeli conduct when viewed in its totality. In this section, the Special Rapporteur applies the framework set out above to the totality of conduct targeting the totality of Palestinians, in the totality of the occupied

Palestinian territory ("totality triple lens"). She then analyses specific components of Israeli conduct: the broader context of the political project of Israel in the region; the nature of the destruction inflicted on the Palestinian people; and the motives obscuring the specific intent itself.

## A. Totality of the land: "Greater Israel"

55. The ambition for a "Greater Israel" (*Eretz Yisrael*), consolidating Jewish sovereignty over the territory now comprising both Israel and the occupied Palestinian territory, has been a long-standing goal since the very inception of the Zionist project and before Israel existed. The legally recognized right to self-determination of Palestinians being tied to that land, together with their large presence, have represented both legal and demographic impediments to the realization of "Greater Israel".

56. Successive Governments have pursued this goal, predicated on the erasure of the Indigenous Palestinian people. Even after the Oslo Accords, which marked international support for a two-State solution, the plan was advanced. Since then, Israeli colonies have increased from 128 to 358, and settler numbers have grown from 256,400 to 714,600. The 2018 Nation State Law asserted exclusive Jewish sovereignty over "Eretz Yisrael" and "Jewish settlement" in that area as a national priority. On 28 December 2022, the current Government of Israel announced its plan to expand the colonies in the West Bank and aggressively advanced substantial land confiscation and settlement expansion. In September 2023, before the General Assembly, Prime Minister Netanyahu exhibited a map of Israel erasing the occupied Palestinian territory and superimposing Israel.

57. The cultivation of a political doctrine that frames Palestinian assertions of self-determination as a security threat to Israel has served to legitimize permanent occupation. The deliberate dehumanization of the Palestinians has accompanied systematic ethnic purges from the period 1947–1949 to today. Ideological hatred of Palestinians as such has pervaded segments of society and the Israeli State apparatus.

58. Meanwhile, despite the oppression, Palestinians refuse to leave the land, and in fact the population has grown.

The increasing risk of a majority-Jewish State becoming unachievable has progressively made destruction an unavoidable part of the process.

59. The events of 7 October provided the impetus to advance towards the goal of a "Greater Israel". Calls for the displacement of Palestinians into the Arab world, amid conquest, colonization and annexation, grew. The leaked Ministry of Intelligence of Israel "concept paper" from October 2023 outlining the expulsion of the entire Gaza population to Egypt, alongside widespread and explicit support within the governing coalition, identifies an opportunity to recolonize Gaza, which the Government seized, taking advantage of the fog of war. In parallel in the West Bank, following 7 October, annexation and colony construction intensified.

60. The State's intent to destroy, expressed in various statements and plans, and inferable from conduct considered in context, has gradually become more recognizable. This conduct had already, prior to 7 October, had the effect of "a cumulative, multilayered and intergenerational impact on the Palestinian society, economy and environment and [had caused] the deterioration of the living conditions of the Palestinians".

61. The violence and trauma suffered by the Israelis on 7 October deepened collective animosity, and calls for annihilation grew. In a manner reminiscent of other genocides, the ensuing vengeful atmosphere prepared the soldiers to become "willing executioners" of the heinous tasks required of them. An opportunity presented itself to sever Palestinian connection to the land, with foreseeable consequences for their Palestinian existence, as outlined below.

## B. Totality of the group: destruction of the Palestinian people

62. Since 7 October 2023, the decimation of Palestinian human life has been swift and extensive. Amid mass killings, eradication of family lines, large-scale targeting of children and torture, the occupied Palestinian territory is being intentionally rendered unliveable – one home, school, church, mosque, hospital, neighbourhood, community, at a time. Spreading from Gaza to the West Bank, calculated destruction

reveals a deliberate campaign of connected incidents, which must be considered cumulatively.

63. Israel has pursued a pattern of conduct "deliberately inflicting on the group conditions of life calculated to bring about its physical destruction", as evidenced by the systematic destruction of already precarious life-sustaining healthcare, food security and Water, Sanitation and Hygiene for All (WASH) infrastructure. Although varying in intensity across the occupied territory, in Gaza this destructive violence has already led to starvation, epidemics and forced displacement with no possibility of safe return – as expressly intended. The destruction of infrastructure across the occupied Palestinian territory imperils the long-term survival of the group. The deliberate degradation of public health is a technique of genocide "by attrition". More than 500,000 children with no schooling and 88,000 students without universities are doomed to dire outcomes.

64. For Palestinians, further layers of agony and forced displacement aggravate their inherited trauma and psychological vulnerability as Nakba survivors. Months of relentless shunting of weakened humans from one unsafe area to another – fleeing bombs and bullets, with minimal chances of escape, amid loss, fear and grief, and with little access to shelter, clean water, food and healthcare – have inflicted incalculable harm, especially on children. The movement of displaced Palestinians resembles the death marches of past genocides, and the Nakba. Forced displacement severs connection with the land, undermining food sovereignty and cultural belonging, and triggering further displacement. Communal bonds are broken, the social fabric shredded and reserves of resilience depleted. Systematic forced displacement contributes to "the destruction of the spirit, of the will to live, and of life itself".

65. As was foreseeable, the overall conduct of Israel post-7 October has inflicted severe psychological harm on all Palestinians, both direct victims and those witnessing in exile. The overall aim is to humiliate and degrade Palestinians as a whole. Prisoners stripped and sadistically tortured en masse; bodies of adults and children piled up and decomposing in the street; survivors forced to eat animal food and grass and drink seawater or even sewage; the maiming

of thousands, including young children left limbless before they could even crawl; the destruction of homes and violation of intimate life; having absolutely nothing to return to. Mass graves and the exhumation and relocation of bodies are specific acts of desecration, which themselves can suggest genocidal intent. Combined, these acts go far beyond what international jurisprudence recognizes as "step[s] in the process of destruction of the ... group". The pain and loss will impact generations to come.

66. Genocide could manifest in the targeting of members of the same group in different parts of their territory, through acts of varying intensity. In the background, Palestinians inside Israel ("the enemies within") have also experienced suppression. The relentless attacks against the United Nations, and, in particular, UNRWA, threaten the socioeconomic lifelines of millions of Palestinian refugees across the broader region, and cannot be ignored.

67. The destructive consequences of Israeli conduct reverberate well beyond the Gaza epicentre, as the same patterns of genocidal conduct have begun to appear in the West Bank. The only inference to be reasonably drawn from all this is of a clear intention to attack "the group's capacity to renew itself, and hence to ensure its long-term survival".

## C. Totality of the conduct: genocidal intent rationalized as self-defence

68. In the face of such wholesale destruction, the stated goals of Israel, accepted by some States, remain "to eradicate Hamas" and "bring the hostages home". Neither of these goals, or motives, preclude a finding of genocidal intent as the only reasonable inference to be drawn. Instead, both motives, together and disjunctively, substantiate the genocidal intent.

69. History reveals that:
    (a) As recognized in the jurisprudence, genocide may occur in the context of armed conflict. As Judge Trindade elaborated: "perpetrators of genocide will almost always allege that ... their actions were taken 'pursuant to an ongoing military conflict'; yet, 'genocide may be a means for achieving military objectives just as readily as military conflict may be a means for instigating a genocidal plan';"

(b) Different underlying motives do not displace genocidal intent. As observed by Judge Bhandari, "genocidal *intent* may exist *simultaneously* with other, *ulterior motives*".
In international criminal jurisprudence, intent (the aim to
achieve a criminal result: destruction of the group) is distin-
guished from motive (the reasons behind an action: hatred,
revenge/collective punishment, personal political agendas,
alleged threat). Although motive is usually irrelevant in
criminal law, it can reveal intent.

70. Post-7 October, Israel has framed its military operations in
    Gaza as a war of self-defence and counter-terrorism against
    a terrorist group. However, it is well established that
    Israel cannot legitimately invoke self-defence against the
    population under its occupation. The occupying Power must
    protect, not target, the occupied people. In the context of Israel
    ignoring the ICJ directive to end the unlawful occupation, the
    aim to eradicate resistance contradicts the rights to self-de-
    termination and to resist an oppressive regime, protected by
    customary international law. It also portrays the entire popu-
    lation as engaged in resistance and therefore eliminable. By
    continuing to suppress the right to self-determination, Israel
    is replicating historical instances in which self-defence,
    counter-insurgency or counter-terrorism were used to jus-
    tify destruction of the group, leading to genocide.

71. With the dehumanization of Palestinians reaching a peak,
    the world has become inured to the individual and collective
    toll of their devastation. In Gaza, Israel has targeted both
    military operatives and ordinary civilians, including from
    local governance structures and civil servants. Expanding
    full-scale military operations to the West Bank further ex-
    poses an aim to target Palestinians beyond Hamas.

72. As the President of Israel, Isaac Herzog, announced, Israel
    has operated on the basis that "it is an entire nation out
    there that is responsible". The entire population – deemed
    "non-innocent" and "not uninvolved" by Israel – has
    been subject to indiscriminate and disproportionate attacks.
    Scorched-earth tactics have spread terror among civilians,
    far exceeding the bounds of legitimate force. Continual,
    unproven attributions of Hamas affiliation and allegations of
    "human shielding" in almost every assault help disguise
    the systematic targeting of civilians, de facto erasing Pales-

tinian civilian-ness altogether. The resulting incommensurate losses sustained by Palestinians compared with Israeli losses, viewed in the context of the vastly superior Israeli military capabilities, suggest an intent other than that claimed.

73. The disturbing frequency and callousness of the killing of people known to be civilians are "emblematic of the systematic nature" of a destructive intent. Six- year-old Hind Rajab, killed with 355 bullets after pleading for help for hours; the fatal mauling by dogs of Muhammed Bhar, who had Down's Syndrome; the execution of Atta Ibrahim Al-Muqaid, an older deaf man, in his home, later bragged about by his killer and other soldiers on social media; the premature babies deliberately left to die a slow death and decompose in the intensive care unit at Al-Nasr Hospital; the elderly man, Bashir Hajji, killed en route to southern Gaza after appearing in a propaganda photograph of a "safe corridor"; Abu al-Ola, the handcuffed hostage shot by a sniper after being sent into Nasser Hospital with evacuation orders. When the dust settles on Gaza, the true extent of the horror experienced by Palestinians will become known.

74. The second stated goal of Israel is to rescue Israeli hostages. This claim has been undermined by the harm caused by Israel to the hostages themselves: more have been killed by indiscriminate Israeli bombing or friendly fire than rescued. Sabotaging the ceasefire negotiations resulted in hostage deaths. The words and conduct of Israeli high-ranking officials, including Prime Minister Netanyahu, indicate that regaining and retaining control over Gaza's territory has overridden the release of hostages as a priority.

# VI. Understanding genocidal intent within a State

75. Accountability for genocide cannot be limited to criminal responsibility of individuals, who are to be judged in criminal trials with due process guarantees. It would be a tragic paradox if the rights of victims were subordinated to the guarantees afforded to alleged perpetrators and their Governments. Furthermore, the responsibility of the State must be assessed in its own right. The moment one genocidal act

occurs and the special intent manifests, this signals that genocide is taking place. This is the moment to intervene – early intervention being the only way to prevent more atrocities that will scar human history.

76. State responsibility entails actions and omissions that lead to genocide. Conduct attributable to the State includes executive, legislative, judicial or any other functions or actions carried out by State organs and legal persons with government authority (even *ultra vires* actions). This includes military personnel and persons acting under instructions or control of a State, or conduct acknowledged by the State as its own. All such conduct should be assessed in its totality.

77. A State is obliged to prevent, to not commit and to punish genocide. According to ICJ, the State obligation to prevent genocide arises as soon as the State becomes aware, or should reasonably be aware, of a "serious risk of genocide", and specifically on the emergence of a reasonable suspicion that genocidal intent has formed within the State apparatus. The State is obliged to investigate and prosecute those suspected of committing genocide and ancillary offences of direct and public incitement, attempt, aid and assist and conspiracy. Knowing the risk of genocide, but failing to act to prevent or to take action to punish these preparatory acts, should be taken as indication of genocidal intent.

78. In autocratic governance systems, checks and balances to curb genocidal conduct are likely either non-existent or non-functioning. Conversely, in a State that claims to have a rule of law system, the legislature, executive or judiciary should be able to curb excesses (generally crimes in and of themselves) that may escalate into genocide. All State organs understand their function as a check on the excesses of others – primarily the executive's. The failure of an apparent rule of law State apparatus to fulfil those obligations, knowing what the consequences will be, must be seen as an integral part of the totality of conduct that should be assessed when determining State genocidal intent.

79. Acts or omissions of a State may contribute to "the opportunity to commit genocide", a circumstantial factor that ICJ has considered when assessing inferences to be drawn. Jurisprudence also recognizes that "the prevailing atmosphere of impunity" and "the encouragement of the authorities" may increase the possibility of crimes leading to genocide.

80. A conservative assessment would lead to the conclusion that, at a minimum, the orders of ICJ on 26 January 2024 should have triggered this duty to act. The Court had specifically instructed Israel to:

- Refrain from further acts that may amount to genocide

- Prevent and punish genocidal incitement

- Allow humanitarian assistance

- Preserve evidence

- Submit a report to the Court detailing steps taken to implement the ruling within one month

81. Instead, genocidal violence continued in Gaza with serious risk of expanding to the West Bank amid increasing genocidal incitement, as demonstrated in section III of the present report. No one has been investigated or prosecuted, let alone punished. Immediately after the Court issued provisional measures, Israel launched an unsubstantiated campaign against UNRWA, which jeopardized the fragile lifelines necessary for humanitarian assistance in Gaza. The following examples offer a snapshot of how various arms of the State have participated in forming the State's intent:

(a) Statements made by the political-military leadership must be adjudicated as evidence of both direct intent and part of the totality of conduct from which intent is inferable. Direct orders at the highest levels of Israeli leadership, as meticulously documented by South Africa, are the hallmark of the genocide in Gaza. These genocidal statements and incitements have continued unabated throughout the past year and echoed at all levels of the military structure. Relentless genocidal incitement by Israeli officials hastened the "normalization" of exterminatory violence;

(b) The members of the Security and War Cabinets of Israel, and other ministers, have issued such genocidal statements and used their ministerial responsibilities to implement their words, authorizing the various genocidal acts in Gaza, such as starvation, obstruction of humanitarian assistance and creation of conditions of life that would lead to destruction;

(c) The Knesset has fully supported the Government and provided a platform for utterly dehumanizing debates concerning Palestinians. The Deputy Speaker declared on 8 Oc-

tober 2023, "Now we all have one common goal – erasing
the Gaza Strip from the face of the Earth". The Knesset has
passed emergency laws, amendments and repeated extensions
to the *Detention of Unlawful Combatants Law*, thereby fa-
cilitating the imposition of even more deplorable conditions
on Palestinian detainees; condoned torture, including rape
of Palestinian detainees (derogatively called "Nukhba"), and
approved budgets for military and colony expansion. In July
2024, the Knesset voted against the two-State solution;

(d) The Attorney General has failed to investigate and
prosecute acts preparatory to and associated with genocide,
such as war crimes, torture and starvation, and to implement the provisional measures against genocidal incitement,
while pursuing those "inciting" support for Palestinian resistance. This draws on and consolidates the long-standing
environment of impunity  recognized by ICJ;

(e) The judiciary has failed to impose limitations on criminal conduct and administrative excesses, or enforce any
accountability, in almost 12 months, effectively granting
impunity to public officials, military personnel and settlers. Courts dismissed a petition regarding Palestinian prison
conditions and rejected an appeal relating to media access
to Gaza. Following the ICJ provisional measures order, the
High Court did agree to hear a petition on humanitarian
aid to Gaza in March 2024, and others on torture and
conditions of detention. However, no persons or institutions
have been held accountable;

(f) The role of the Israeli media in inciting this genocide, by helping to foster an unchecked genocidal climate,
ought to be examined judicially – as has occurred in other
contexts. Compounding decades of dehumanization of the
Palestinians, the media have platformed proponents of genocide and debates legitimating their brutalization, and have
withheld the facts from the Israeli public. State actions have
exacerbated the situation, including heavy military censorship, the killing of 111 Palestinian journalists, denial of entry
to foreign journalists to Gaza and the forced closure of Al Jazeera's offices in Israel and the West Bank. Meanwhile, Israeli
regulatory agencies have neither exercised their authority
to revoke  broadcast licences nor issued financial sanctions
against those using or amplifying genocidal statements.

82. The State of Israel is predicated on the goal of Palestin-

ian erasure; its entire political system is directed towards this goal. State structures have historically architected the oppression of Palestinians; now its institutions, failing to function as a bulwark, are together advancing the course of the current catastrophe.

# VII. Conclusions

83. **The Gaza genocide is a tragedy foretold, and one that risks expanding to other Palestinians under Israeli rule. Since its establishment, Israel has treated The occupied people as a hated encumbrance and threat to be eradicated, subjecting millions of Palestinians, for generations, to everyday indignities, mass killing, mass incarceration, forced displacement, racial segregation and apartheid. Advancing its goal of "Greater Israel" threatens to erase the Indigenous Palestinian population.**

84. **Obscured by false Israeli narratives of a war waged in "self-defence", the genocidal conduct of Israel must be viewed within a broader context, as numerous actions (totality of conduct) jointly targeting the Palestinians as such (totality of a people) across the entire territory where they reside (totality of the land), in furtherance of the political ambitions of Israel for sovereignty over the whole of former Mandatory Palestine. Today, the genocide of the Palestinians appears to be the means to an end: the complete removal or eradication of Palestinians from the land so integral to their identity, and which is illegally and openly coveted by Israel.**

85. **Statements and actions by Israeli leaders reflect a genocidal intent and conduct; they have often used the Biblical story of Amalek to justify the extermination of "the Gazans", erasing Gaza and violently displacing Palestinians, thereby casting Palestinians as a whole as legitimate targets.**

86. **Individuals clearly identifiable as perpetrators should be prosecuted. However, it is the entire State apparatus that has engineered, articulated and executed genocidal violence, through acts which in their totality may lead to the destruction of the Palestinian people. This must stop;**

urgent action is required to ensure the full application of the Genocide Convention and full protection of the Palestinians.

87. This ongoing genocide is doubtlessly the consequence of the exceptional status and protracted impunity that has been afforded to Israel. Israel has systematically and flagrantly violated international law, including Security Council resolutions and ICJ orders. This has emboldened the hubris of Israel and its defiance of international law. As the ICC Prosecutor has warned, "if we do not demonstrate our willingness to apply the law equally, if it is seen as applied selectively, we will be creating the conditions of its complete collapse. This is the true risk we face at this perilous moment."

88. As the world watches the first live-streamed settler-colonial genocide, only justice can heal the wounds that political expedience has allowed to fester. The devastation of so many lives is an outrage to humanity and all that international law stands for.

# VIII.    Recommendations

89. The current genocide is part of a century-long project of eliminatory settler- colonialism in Palestine, a stain on the international system and humanity, which must be ended, investigated and prosecuted.

90. The Special Rapporteur reminds all States of their legal obligation to act on their due diligence duties given the clearly serious risk of continuous breach of the Genocide Convention and Geneva Conventions, and urges States to consider and reach an urgent public determination as to what levers and tools each State has at its disposal to ameliorate that risk, whether acting alone or with other States, including at the United Nations; and to explain to the public and the international community the steps which it has taken and why.

91. Whether in compliance with the above due diligence duties or otherwise, the Special Rapporteur urges Member States to:
    (a) Use all their political leverage – commencing with

a full arms embargo and sanctions – so that Israel stops the assault against the Palestinians, accepts a ceasefire and fully withdraws from the occupied Palestinian territory in line with the ICJ Advisory Opinion of 19 July 2024;

(b) Formally recognize Israel as an apartheid State and persistent violator of international law, reactivating the Special Committee Against Apartheid to comprehensively address the situation in Palestine, and warn Israel of possible suspension of its membership under Article 6 of the Charter of the United Nations;

(c) Support the deployment of an international protective presence throughout the occupied Palestinian territory;

(d) Develop a protective framework for Palestinians displaced outside Gaza, in line with international human rights and refugee law, while fully preserving their right to return;

(e) Support independent and thorough investigation(s) of criminal conduct, including genocide and apartheid, including through the application in national courts of universal jurisdiction over those suspected of such criminal conduct, including all relevant ancillary offences;

(f) Investigate and prosecute corporate entities and dual citizens involved in crimes in the occupied Palestinian territory, including soldiers, mercenaries and settlers;

(g) Ensure unhindered humanitarian assistance to Gaza and full financing and protection of UNRWA, including from attacks on its premises and personnel and from libellous smear campaigns, and ensure the continuity of its mandate in all fields.

1.  The Special Rapporteur urges the ICC Prosecutor to investigate the commission of the crimes of genocide and apartheid by Israel, and investigate other prominent individuals mentioned in the present report.

1.  The Special Rapporteur urges the Independent International Commission of Inquiry on the Occupied Palestinian Territory, including East Jerusalem, and

Israel to investigate the broader context of eliminatory intent and practices of Israel against all
Palestinians (triple lens test), including those with
Israeli citizenship and the refugees, and recent acts
of genocide.

# INDEX